A Woman's Journey through Ruth

8 Lessons on Love Exclusively for Women

Dee Brestin

Chariot Victor Publishing
A Division of Cook Communications

Titles by Dee Brestin

From Chariot Victor

The Friendships of Women
The Friendships of Women Workbook
We Are Sisters
The Joy of Women's Friendships
The Joy of Eating Right
The Joy of Hospitality
A Woman of Joy
A Woman of Value
A Woman of Insight
A Woman's Journey through Luke
A Woman's Journey through Ruth
A Woman's Journey through Esther

Fisherman Bible Study Guides

(Harold Shaw Publishers)
Proverbs and Parables
Ecclesiastes
Examining the Claims of Christ (John 1–5)
1, 2 Peter and Jude
How Should a Christian Live? (1, 2, 3 John)
Higher Ground
Building Your House on the Lord
Friendship

From Moody Press

Believer's Lifesystem—Women's Edition Bible Study

Chariot Victor Publishing
A division of Cook Communications, Colorado Springs, Colorado 80918
Cook Communications, Paris, Ontario
Kingsway Communications, Eastbourne, England

Editors: Barbara Williams and Dorian Coover-Cox
Design: Bill Gray
Cover Photo: Kevin Buckley

1 2 3 4 5 6 7 8 9 10 Printing/Year 02 01 00 99 98

Contents

How I Thank God For:

My Editors:
Dorian Coover-Cox who teaches Old Testament at Dallas Theological Seminary, for her knowledge, discernment, and perspective as a godly woman.

Barb Williams for her care with artwork and with every jot, tittle, and comma.

My Brothers in Christ at Chariot Victor:
especially and always, Greg Clouse.

Bill Gray, for such striking covers for this series.

My Assistant:
Gay Tillotson, whose energy, enthusiasm, insight, and administrative skill have made us an Ecclesiastes 4:9-10 team.

My Sisters in Christ, Including:
the reflective and diligent women of Sonrise Bible Studies who tested this guide and vulnerably allowed me to read their answers.

my prayer support team to whom I attribute the wonderful sense I have had of God's hand upon me.

My Family, Including:
all of our children for their prayers and support.

and my absolutely amazing and godly husband, Steve, who is so supportive, encouraging, insightful, and dear.

Introduction

This is one in a series of guides written especially for women. This series would be incomplete without the two books in the Bible named for women: Ruth and Esther. While there are life-changing principles in Ruth and Esther for both genders, there are also messages that are uniquely for women.

> *SO, SISTERS, PLEASE HEAR THIS:*
>
> *THE BOOKS OF RUTH AND ESTHER ARE GOD'S SPECIAL GIFTS TO US.*
>
> *TREASURE THEM. UNWRAP THEM SLOWLY.*
>
> *ALLOW HIS SPIRIT TO ETCH THEIR TRUTHS UPON YOUR HEART.*

The Book of Ruth has often been called the book of *hesed* or unfailing love. Through this little book of love I have heard my Heavenly Father say:

> *I love you. Look for Me in the figure of Boaz. As he reached out to Ruth and protected her, provided for her, and met her need, so I long to do the same for you.*
>
> *When your relationship with Me is right, I can transform your relationship with others.*
>
> *I made you. Therefore I understand your feminine gifts and I long to show you how to use them redemptively. Naomi will show you how to be a good mother-in-law. Ruth will show you how to be a good daughter-in-law, an amazing friend, and a woman of noble character.*
>
> *Many have minimized women's friendships, saying they are shallow and catty. My little Book of Ruth stands against that lie, showing the power that can be released through the love and faith of women.*

Studying the Book of Ruth also illustrates the need for women to be taught by women, as Titus 2 exhorts. Commentaries can be very helpful, but they are almost always from the life experience and perspective of a male. And while I have drawn upon the wisdom of some very gifted men, and I in no way minimize their contributions, I have also found helpful resources on Ruth written by women. Because they share much of your life experience and perspective, I know they will open new vistas for you. As Jan Titterington said, in commenting on the Book of Ruth: "Just as the hand needs the eye, it needs the other hand."[1] We need both men and women for completion in the body of Christ.

Instructions for Preparation and Discussion

One of the repeated images in the Book of Ruth is that of Ruth filling the empty arms of her mother-in-law. I am praying you will do that for one another in this study by being faithful with the following:

1.   Do your homework! Each day, same time, same place, to establish a habit. Each day, ask God to speak to you through His Word. Jesus says that "out of the overflow of our hearts" we speak. If you come to the study overflowing with insights from Ruth, you will fill your sisters' cups.

2.   Get a hymnal as hymns will be suggested to enrich your quiet time. A prayer journal would also be an excellent additional tool. Effective prayer warriors take a few minutes each day to jot down their prayers and then highlight or star the answers.

3.   In the discussion, be sensitive. The naturally talkative women need to exercise control and the shy women need to exercise courage to speak up. One of the reasons God used Ruth so mightily was that she knew when to speak and when to be silent.

4.   Stay on target in the discussions. These lessons can be discussed in ninety minutes. If you don't have that much time, you have two options:

A. Divide the lessons and meet for sixteen weeks. Do that week's prayer exercise both weeks.

B. Do the whole lesson but discuss half the questions.

5.   Follow the instructions for group prayer at the close of each lesson. Keep confidences in the group. One of the beautiful aspects of the Book of Ruth is that the bold prayers offered on behalf of each other are all answered. There is power when we pray together.

CHOOSE THIS DAY WHOM YOU WILL SERVE

At this they wept again.
Then Orpah kissed her mother-in-law
good-by, but Ruth clung to her.
—Ruth 1:14

One

In the Days When the Judges Ruled

Che story of Ruth occurred in the days when the judges ruled, when "every man did that which was right in his own eyes" (Judges 21:25, KJV). Because we are not capable of living righteously apart from God's guidance, those were dark days indeed. Similarly, individuals and nations today who turn away from God become selfish, immoral, and blind.

Yet, even in the darkest of days, God has always had a people, a remnant, a pearl that gleams in the darkness. Naomi, Ruth, and Boaz gleam "like a beautiful pearl against a jet-black background."[2] God longs that we will gleam like that as well. He says:

> Do everything without complaining or arguing, so that you may become blameless and pure, children of God without fault in a crooked and depraved generation, in which you shine like stars in the universe.
> (Philippians 2:14-15)

In order to understand the Book of Ruth, we need to understand the dark days in which Ruth lived and the longing that God had for His people.

Prepare Your Heart to Hear

Before each of the following six devotional times, quiet your heart and ask God to speak to you personally from His Word. In Deuteronomy 6:3 the Lord says: "Hear, O Israel, and be careful to obey that it may go well with you." Substitute your name for "Israel" and resolve to listen.

Memory Work

Over the next three weeks you will memorize Ruth 1:16-17 from the *King James Version.* Begin this week with:

> **And Ruth said: "Entreat me not to leave thee, or to return from following after thee: for whither thou goest, I will go."**

Warm-Up

Share your name and why you came to this group. One of the images in the Book of Ruth is that of Ruth filling her mother-in-law's empty arms. How have women in small group fellowships like this filled up an emptiness in your spirit?

Day 1: Overview

1.   Read all of the Introductory notes. Comment on what stood out to you from:

A. The Introduction (pp. 5-6)

B. The Special Instructions for Preparation and Discussion (p. 7)

C. The Introduction for Chapter One: IN THE DAYS WHEN THE JUDGES RULED (p. 10)

2.   Read through the Book of Ruth. As you do, look for ways Ruth tried to fill Naomi's empty arms. (The book is short—it may take you only ten minutes to read.) What did you see?

Spend five minutes on the memory passage.

Often doing a word at a time will help to cement it in your mind:

Ruth
Ruth 1
Ruth 1:16-17
Ruth 1:16-17 Entreat
Ruth 1:16-17 Entreat me
Ruth 1:16-17 Entreat me not
etc.

Day 2: Famine in the Promised Land?

Famine was common in the dry lands of the ancient Near East, but God had promised that the land He gave His people would be a land flowing with milk and honey. Yet when the Book of Ruth opens, we find a famine in the Promised Land, in *Bethlehem,* which, ironically, means "house of bread."

When trouble comes into our lives, we would be wise to examine our hearts and see if there is any sin in us. Solomon says, in Ecclesiastes 7:14,

When times are good, be happy;
but when times are bad, consider:
God has made the one as well as the other.

Bad times can come to the totally innocent, as they did to Jesus. Righteous people suffer. Sometimes that suffering is due to sin in the world, for the consequences of sin are like an oozing rash, spreading to the guilty *and* the innocent.

Sometimes suffering comes to the righteous because God has a plan that is hidden from their sight. Elizabeth and Zechariah were blameless, we are told, but also barren, because God had a plan to give them a miracle baby in their old age as a sign that "nothing is impossible with God" (Luke 1:37).

But bad times *can* be a result of personal or corporate sin, for we do reap what we sow and God does test His people. That is why we must continually examine our hearts to see if we have wandered into the darkness.

Before God ever brought the Israelites into the Promised Land, He told them clearly how He wanted them to live. Obedience would bring plenty, disobedience would bring famine.

3. In Ruth 1:1, find these facts:
    A. When did the story of Ruth take place?

    B. What was happening in the Promised Land?

    C. How did this family respond to the famine?

Read Deuteronomy 7:1-16.

4. In Deuteronomy 7:1-4, why does God tell the Israelites not to intermarry with the people of the nations He would drive out of the Promised Land?

5. The above warning is often repeated in Scripture (1 Kings 11:1-4; 1 Corinthians 7:39; 2 Corinthians 6:14). How do both Scripture and life show this commandment to be wise?

    What are some specific things that a mother can do while her children are young to impress this wisdom on their hearts?

    How have you seen godly parents guide and protect their teens from a foolish choice in marriage? (Dating age? Courtship? Prayer?)

6.   In Deuteronomy 7:12-16, what promises does God make to the Israelites? What are the conditions?

Read Deuteronomy 11:8-21.

7.   How does God describe the Promised Land in verse 9? How is it going to be different from Egypt? (verses 10-12)

8.   What else does God tell the Israelites to do in Deuteronomy 11:18-21?

These verses apply to all believing adults. How are you obeying verse 19?

9.   Joshua died just before the days of the judges began. What warnings, similar to the warnings of Moses, did he give?
    A. Joshua 23:12-13

    B. Joshua 23:14-16

As you will see, the Israelites did not obey Moses or Joshua. They married unbelievers, they failed to pass on the truths of God to their children, and that generation "knew neither the Lord nor what He had done for Israel" (Judges 2:10).

Read Judges 2:8-13.

10. What phrases describe the disobedience of the Israelites after Joshua's death?

Even in the darkest of days, God will hear the cry of an individual or a nation that is truly brokenhearted and repentant. One of the themes of the Book of Judges is the compassion of God. His concern and love for Israel is deep, He is always open to their cries, always ready to send a deliverer. When a nation or an individual sincerely cries out to God, He will hear.

11. How do the following passages say God will respond when an individual repents for personal sin or a body of people repents for corporate sin?
    A. 1 John 1:9

    B. 2 Chronicles 7:13-14

12. Why do you think there was a famine in the opening of Ruth?

    How do you think God wanted His people to respond?

13. When trouble comes into our lives, why should we consider whether it could be a result of personal or corporate sin?

When A.W. Tozer had his daily time with the Lord, he always used a Bible and a hymnal. Every home needs both. Today, turn to one of the following songs in your hymnal and sing it reflectively: "Cleanse Me" or "Change My Heart, O God."

Day 3: The Downward Cycle of Sin

If we do not repent of sin, it grips our hearts and enslaves us. In the days of the judges, the Israelites repeatedly rebelled against the Lord and fell under the power of an invading nation. Then God would hear their cries. In His mercy He would send a "judge," a "deliverer." The Israelites would be rescued and a time of peace would follow.

But then, in that time of peace, they would again rebel against the Lord, and the cycle would repeat. This happens seven times in the Book of Judges and each time they would sink to deeper depths. In *The Bible Reader's Companion*, Larry Richards characterizes the cycles in this way:

1: SIN   2: SERVITUDE   3: SUPPLICATION   4: SALVATION   5: SILENCE[3]

14. In Judges 3:7-11, trace the first cycle through sin, servitude, supplication, salvation, and silence.

15. Read Judges 3:12-30.
    A. Describe how the cycle repeats.

B. How does Ehud use treachery to assassinate the king of Moab?

This rather strange story of the assassination of the fat king of Moab by a left-handed deliverer is significant to our study of Ruth in that it graphically pictures some of the material blessings of the Moabites which were lacking among the Israelites. Kenneth R.R. Gros Louis says:

> *Eglon, we are told, is a very fat man, a detail which characterizes his sumptuous style of living and which also underlines the plight of the Israelites.*
>
> *. . . the Moabite king is relaxing "in his cool roof chamber," attended by servants. The one small detail opens up for us the vast differences between the lives of the Moabites and the conquered Israelites—inside versus outside, cool versus hot, fatness versus leanness, palms versus the hills.*[4]

16. In Judges 6:27-30, how did the Israelites respond when Gideon obeyed the Lord and tore down their altar to Baal?

Many believe the Book of Ruth took place in the days of Gideon, for there was a famine at that time.

17. Though generally the Israelites were far from God, as evidenced by the above, there was a remnant. How do you see this in Gideon's father Joash in Judges 6:31?

18. In the following passages concerning Samson, what can you discern about his motivations in life?
    A. Judges 14:1-3

B. Judges 16:1

C. Judges 16:4-5 (Extra credit! Read the whole chapter!)

Even the deliverers, like the people they were delivering, were not particularly admirable. They were often treacherous, weak in faith and in moral fiber. They reflect the depravity of Israel. The One who truly delivered Israel through these seven cycles was God, though He used the tarnished and cracked vessels of men like Ehud and Samson. Israel had lost its godly perspective.

19. Often what we think we need for fulfillment is not what we need at all. We do not need a sumptuous summer palace where servants fan us. Jesus said not to be concerned about food and clothes but about God's kingdom and His righteousness. How could you apply this to your life today?

Review your memory work.

Ruth 1:16-17 is also symbolic of the depth of commitment God wants from us.

Day 4: The Frog in the Kettle

Drop a frog into boiling water and he'll hop out. But drop him in cold water, warm it slowly, and he will sit there, unaware, and die. So it is with the downward cycles of sin. We are unaware of how hot the water has become and of the wrath we have provoked in a holy God.

Read Judges 19.

20. In Judges 17–18, an Israelite leaves the Promised Land and faces tragedy. Explain how this happens again in Judges 19.

Those familiar with these two incidents in Judges would have a sense of apprehension when they read, in the opening of Ruth, of an Israelite choosing to leave the Promised Land.

21. Briefly describe the depths of sin in Judges 19.

> . . . what gradual descents a man may glide from one stage of wickedness to another, till, under favouring circumstances, he reaches a depth of vileness which at one time would have seemed impossible. . . . At each successive stage of descent there is less shock to the weakened moral sense. . . . The sin appears less odious, and the resisting power is less strong.
>
> . . .It is in steady resistance to the first beginnings of sin, and in steadfast cleaving to God, that man's safety lies. It is in the maintenance of religion that the safety of society consists. Without the fear of God man would soon become a devil, and earth would become a hell.
> Dr. A.C. Hervey[5]

22. The horrible story above is meant to be a warning. List some things in your nation that would have been shocking a generation ago but today are accepted.

Now consider your life. Are there videos you are renting or books you are reading which would have shocked you once? If so, how could you leap out of the kettle now, before it is too late?

Personal Action Assignment
Spend time in personal confession and confession for your nation.

Review your memory passage.

Day 5: They Went to Live for a While in Moab

When a famine came to Bethlehem, Elimelech could look across the Salt Sea to the greener hills of Moab. Although there were times of war between Moab and Israel, basically the Moabites were peaceful. Also, because Israel had become so depraved, this pagan nation didn't seem too different.

Archeologists[6] have discovered that the Israelites and Moabites had much in common including similar pottery, house styles, scripts, and languages. The discovery of the Moabite Stone[7] corroborated the incident recorded in 2 Kings which tells how King Mesha "took his firstborn son, who was to succeed him as king, and offered him as a sacrifice on the city wall" (2 Kings 3:27).

Among other gods, the Moabites worshiped Chemosh, and their worship involved sexual immorality.[8] The Moabites would send their daughters to cultivate friendly relations with the Israelites and then entice them to their idolatrous services.[9]

It was to this land that Elimelech took his wife and his two sons of marrying age.

23. Read Genesis 19:30-37 and explain the origin of the Moabites.

24. Read Numbers 25 and describe:
   A. Why did God become angry with the men of Israel? (verses 1-3)

   B. How did an Israelite show his lack of regard for God? (verse 6)

   C. What did Phinehas do and what was the result? (verses 7-13)

Sexual acts as part of worship?[10] It seems very strange indeed. But the Moabites believed that when cosmic deities had intercourse, it gave birth to new life in the land, to green hills and lush crops. The worshipers would perform on earth, often on hills in full view of the gods, the acts they wished the gods to imitate in heaven. So the Moabite women lured the Israelite men not only through sexual temptation, but through the hope that maybe this really would help their land produce better crops.

25. Though we don't worship Chemosh or Baal, we have other idols. We often fail to cling to the only God who can help. What "gods" do you run to other than the one true God for love or comfort? Why is this foolish?

26. God is angry when His children are unfaithful and He is also angry toward those who tempt them to be unfaithful. What pronouncement did God make concerning the Moabites?
   A. Deuteronomy 23:3

   B. Nehemiah 13:1

Day 6: Ruth Was a Moabitess

Ruth, a Moabitess, not only enters into the assembly of the Lord, but becomes the great grandmother of King David and the ancestor of the Messiah. Why? When we put our faith in the one true God, our past is wiped away and we have a new identity.

Review your memory passage.

27. How does 2 Corinthians 5:17 show what happens to a person who puts her trust in the Lord?

   Have you put your trust in Jesus Christ? If so, share in a sentence how it happened.

What are some ways you are aware that He has made you a new creation?

In your personal quiet time sing, "To God Be the Glory."

28. Read Ruth 1:1 again and share any new insight you have, because of this lesson, on the following phrases:
    A. In the days when the judges ruled

    B. there was a famine in the land

    C. and a man from Bethlehem in Judah, together with his wife and two sons, went to live for a while in the country of Moab.

29. What impressed you personally from this lesson? How do you think God would have you apply it to your life? (If time permits, hear from everyone on this, giving women the freedom to pass.)

Prayer Time
Today, for your first time, have the discussion leader close in prayer.

Two

Love in a Time of Famine

It is Thanksgiving weekend and our family has been celebrating the "harvest," the many blessings God has bestowed on us. Early this morning the beauty of the earth greeted us as the rising sun turned the Nebraska sky crimson and purple. My husband and I stood on the back porch in our flannel robes, marveling at the sight and, with a little encouragement from me, sang: "Holy, Holy, Holy." Material blessings abound: a warm home with a fire flickering in the fireplace; turkey, dressing, and fragrant pumpkin pie. The joy of human love fills our hearts as adult children come home and we cradle our newborn grandson, Simeon: pink, perfect, and plump with possibility.

The Book of Ruth is ripe with images of the land and the harvest, as are the Prophets, the Psalms, and the parables of Jesus. Parallels are often drawn between the fruitfulness of the land and the fruitfulness of lives, and between harvesting the land and harvesting souls on earth. The psalmist compares the godly to a tree planted by rivers of water and the ungodly to the chaff which the wind blows away (Psalm 1). Intriguingly, the climax of the Book of Ruth occurs at the threshing floor, where the grain was lifted with forks and thrown to the night wind so that the chaff could be blown away. Ruth, steadfast and true, is like pure and wholesome grain.

The choices we make in difficulty reveal the source of our trust. When a famine comes to Bethlehem, Elimelech fled to idol-worshiping Moab and took his family with him. Did Naomi protest? We don't know. Perhaps she did, but it didn't matter. We do know that sometime after they arrived in Moab, Elimelech died.

The two sons took women of Moab as their wives. Did Naomi protest? We don't know. Maybe she did, but it didn't matter. Maybe Mahlon and Kilion were like Samson. They wanted those good-looking women and it didn't matter what Mom or God thought.

We do know that Ruth and Orpah loved Naomi. And despite all the pain she experienced, she showed them love. The following years were barren years. Neither girl conceived a baby. But Naomi stood by their sides. She never called them her daughters-in-law. She called them her daughters.

Then, at the end of ten years, the two sons died. The final blow. The place of refuge became a place of death. Yet even in the midst of Naomi's deepest pain, she prayed for her daughters, seeking what she believed to be their best. Through her blinding tears she praised them and prayed that "Yahweh" would show them unfailing love by giving them rest in the home of another husband.

It's easy to love people when things are going well: when it's summertime and the fruit is on the vine, when your health is good, when you have a loving husband to support you, and when your son brings home your dream daughter-in-law who gives you beautiful grandchildren.

It's not so easy when times are hard. You've been uprooted from the Promised Land and taken to a foreign land. Your husband dies and your sons bring home women who worship Chemosh, a god who demands the sacrifice of children. During the following years there are no grandbabies born. Your arms are empty. There is barrenness all around. Life is as gray as sheet-iron.

And yet, even in the worst of times, Naomi shows love. Ruth is the heroine of this book, but she had a model—and that model was Naomi.

Prepare Your Heart to Hear
Before each of the following six devotional times, determine to listen to the Lord. Again and again, as with the Parable of the Sower, Jesus says: "He who has ears to hear, let him hear" (Mark 4:9). Each day, be still, and listen!

Memory Work
Continue memorizing Ruth 1:16-17 (KJV) by completing this portion:

And Ruth said: "Entreat me not to leave thee, or to return from following after thee: for whither thou goest, I will go; and where thou lodgest, I will lodge: thy people shall be my people, and thy God my God."

Warm-Up

Think of a creative picture from the earth to represent each of the following spiritual states:

A hard and barren heart:

A tender and receptive heart:

A divided heart:

A faithful and fruitful heart:

Day 1: Overview

Some have attributed the Book of Ruth to Samuel. On the other hand, "several recent scholars have detected a female perspective in the book which has suggested to them that the author was a woman."[11] In any case, the author was anointed by the Spirit of God and tells the story in a masterful way, taking us through different states of the land and, therefore, of the heart.[12]

It begins with a famine in Bethlehem. Upon moving to Moab, Naomi is hit with one enormous loss after another. However, chapter 1 closes with a whisper of hope as Naomi returns to Bethlehem. The Hebrew word for "return" is related to "repent." Naomi is turning from the land of false gods (who gave her nothing but death) to the Promised Land of Yahweh (from whom all blessings flow). And, symbolically, the two barren widows arrive just "as the barley harvest was beginning" (Ruth 1:22).

The book progresses through harvest, ripe with images of plenty, and then to the threshing floor. The story comes to a swift conclusion with a picture of great fruitfulness and promise in the lives of Ruth, Naomi, and Boaz.

1. Comment on what stood out to you from the Introductory notes:
    A. The Introduction for Chapter Two: LOVE IN A TIME OF FAMINE (pp. 23-24)

    B. Day 1: Overview (p. 25)

2.   Read through the Book of Ruth watching particularly for images of barrenness or fruitfulness, of harvest, of threshing, and of rest. What do you find?

Ruth 1:

Ruth 2:

Ruth 3:

Ruth 4:

Spend five minutes on your memory passage.

The following beloved Thanksgiving song includes images of the land and of our hearts. Sing "Come, Ye Thankful People" to the Lord and ask Him to grant that you will be pure and wholesome grain.

Come, Ye Thankful People

Come, ye thankful people, come, raise the song of harvest home:
All is safely gathered in, ere the winter storms begin;
God, our Maker, doth provide for our wants to be supplied:
Come to God's own temple, come, raise the song of harvest home.

All the world is God's own field, fruit unto His praise to yield;
Wheat and tares together sown, unto joy or sorrow grown;
First the blade, and then the ear, then the full corn shall appear:
Lord of harvest, grant that we wholesome grain and pure may be.

Even so, Lord, quickly come to Thy final harvest home;
Gather Thou Thy people in, free from sorrow, free from sin;
There, forever purified, in Thy presence to abide:
Come, with all Thine angels, come, raise the glorious harvest home.

Day 2: The Far Country

When there is a famine at home, Elimelech takes his family to the "country of Moab." The Moabites were associated with sin and corruption, and had received God's curse.[13] Moab was not being judged, and the grass was green. (God often lets the children of the world go unreproved in this life.) But God does discipline His children. Instead of submitting to God's discipline, Elimelech fled to Moab's greener grass. Elimelech has often been compared to the prodigal son who journeys to the far country and experiences great sorrow and want.

Read Hebrews 12:4-13 carefully.

3. In the above passage:
    A. Whom does the Lord discipline? (verses 6-8)

    B. What is the purpose of God's discipline? (verses 9-10)

    C. When trials come we can choose to stay close to God or to flee. Why is it difficult to stay close to God? Why is it even more difficult to flee His discipline? (verses 11-13)

4. In your own life, think of a path that is pleasing to God but often seems painful to you. (Getting out of bed to spend time with God, forgiving a wrong . . .) Explain how going your own way will actually be *more* painful in the long run.

    Explain how doing it God's way could lead to "a *harvest* of righteousness."

Read the story of the Prodigal Son in Luke 15:11-31.

5. Describe the son's misery in the far country and the joy upon his return.

What spiritual principle do you see here?

Helmut Thielicke, in The Waiting Father, *explains that repentance, though difficult, always brings joy. "Whenever the New Testament speaks of repentance, always the great joy is in the background. It does not say, 'Repent or hell will swallow you up,' but 'Repent, the kingdom of heaven is at hand.'"*[14]

6.   Describe the misery of Elimelech's family in the far country by looking at words related to death and despair in Ruth 1.

Day 3: Choices

There was a famine in the land, but Matthew Henry comments that not everyone left Bethlehem. Survival was possible. Even if Elimelech had mortgaged all of his property, as Ruth 4:5 leads us to believe, there were laws concerning helping neighbors in need (Leviticus 25:35).[15] This famine probably occurred in the days of Gideon. Food was scarce, but there was food.

Why does the author make a point to tell us that this family was "Ephrathite"? Surely the connection with David is important, for the early readers knew he came from this clan (1 Samuel 17:12). Cyril J. Barber thinks that being an "Ephrathite" was the equivalent of being from a well-established family in Boston, and that Elimelech was fearful of losing his wealth and influence in the community.[16] Perhaps Matthew Henry and Cyril Barber are too hard on Elimelech. However, we can say that Elimelech made a poor choice in taking his family to such an immoral place. Can God bring beauty out of ashes? Yes. But that does not justify a poor choice.

God longs for us to cling to Him in a time of testing rather than escaping to a land of sin and corruption. When we are in the desert of testing, fears overwhelm us and reveal the paucity of our faith! Where is He? Maybe a little chocolate or a trip to the mall would ease our fears and satisfy our souls.

WRONG!

Gwen Shamblin, founder of the Weigh-Down Workshop, says:

The Israelites went in and out of worship to idols. As a result, God would then enslave them to the wicked surrounding countries. After a burdensome and painful enslavement, they would repent and turn their hearts back to the Father, and He would free them. So obedience and freedom go together, as do disobedience and slavery.[17]

7.　In the following passages name the choices that are made. What do you think the person hoped would happen as a result of the choice?
　　A. Ruth 1:1

　　B. Ruth 1:4a (concerning wives)

　　C. Ruth 1:4b (concerning returning to Bethlehem)

The phrase translated "lived there" is much more permanent than the Hebrew phrase used in verse 1 and translated "live for a while." Apparently Elimelech planned to return to the Promised Land, but the sons did not.

　　D. Ruth 1:6

　　E. Ruth 1:14a

　　F. Ruth 1:16-17

Review your memory passage.

8.　How are the words of Joshua in Joshua 24:14-15 exemplified in the choices of Orpah and Ruth?

9.   List some of the choices with which you are faced every day that can lead either to freedom or to slavery.

10. What question did Ruth ask Boaz and how did he respond in Ruth 2:10-12?

From your hymnal sing, "In My Life Lord, Be Glorified."

As you make the right choices today, may you be richly rewarded by the Lord, the God of Israel, under whose wings you have come to take refuge.

Day 4: Not Your Dream Daughter-in-Law

Orpah and Ruth couldn't have been Naomi's dream daughters-in-law. They were Moabitesses who worshiped idols. And yet she has a beautiful relationship with them. She never calls them her daughters-in-law, she calls them *benotai,* my daughters. I suspect Ruth Anna Putnam may be correct when she surmises that Naomi accepted Orpah and Ruth because:

> *Her relationships with her sons mattered to her; she knew that those relationships could be maintained and would continue to grow only if they included the new daughters-in-law. So she suppressed whatever misgivings she had. She welcomed Orpah and Ruth, and together they established relationships based on respect and trust.[18]*

The person with whom your son or daughter falls in love depends a great deal on the model he's seen in you and your husband, the truths from God's Word which have been etched on his heart, and the prayers you have brought before God. I have prayed regularly, from the time our children were little, for their future mates. I have asked God to give each of them a mate who loves the Lord deeply. I know God's Word is clear on this. If believers marry unbelievers, they are bringing PAIN into their lives and into the lives of their children.

However, if any of our children disobey God and marry an unbeliever, I will embrace that son-in-law or daughter-in-law. Naomi has taught me that. I know I will never win them into the kingdom if I, as Gary Smalley and John Trent put it, "shut the door and turn the light out."[19]

However, when our children are young, we *should* instruct them on God's guidelines concerning marriage. And as they grow older, we should, if they are open, continue to give them our earnest prayerful counsel. What should that be?

The Bible is clear on the following. Marriage should occur only between people of the opposite sex. (Leviticus 20:13; Romans 1:24-27). Believers are to marry believers. (We looked at these Scriptures in the last lesson: 1 Kings 11:1-4; 1 Corinthians 7:39; 2 Corinthians 6:14.) Marrying a divorced person is permissible under certain circumstances. Outside of that, there are no restrictions. In Christ we have great freedom. Though you may experience less hardship if you marry someone of like background, there is nothing in Scripture that says we are to marry someone of the same race, social class, age, or denomination. If we insist upon that for our child, we are adding to what God has said, and we may actually be working against God's leading. Our commonality is Christ (not skin color, worship style, age, or income).

Read Genesis 27:46 through Genesis 28:9.
(Canaanite women did not worship the one true God, but rather, worshiped sordid gods, prostitute goddesses, serpents, bulls.)

11.   In what area had Rebekah and Isaac failed to train Esau? (verse 28:8)

What was the result for them and for their son?

In taking his sons to Moab, Elimelech increased the likelihood that his sons would marry Moabitesses. While we cannot take our children out of the world, we are foolish if we blatantly lead them into tempting situations or fail to provide opportunities for them to meet godly young people.

12. How might parents provide opportunities for teens to meet godly people of the opposite sex?

13. In today's society our children may consider marrying someone who is divorced. Scripture permits divorce and grants freedom to remarry in two specific cases. What are they?

    A. Matthew 19:9

    B. 1 Corinthians 7:12-15

One of the best and most scripturally sound books I have read on the subject of divorce and remarriage is Craig Keener's . . . And Marries Another.[20] *Dr. Keener tackles difficult issues with compassion and a deep reverence for God's Word. He believes that Scripture permits divorce and remarriage in the cases of adultery or physical abandonment, and he also believes we have a fresh slate when we come to Christ and thus can remarry even if before knowing Christ we divorced for unscriptural reasons.*

14. Sometimes mothers (or older sisters!) oppose a marriage for unscriptural reasons. In Numbers 12, Miriam opposes the marriage of her brother Moses to a Cushite woman (who may have been black). Miriam's root problem was sibling rivalry (Numbers 12:2), but she expresses it through picking on Moses' new wife! How does God respond to Miriam? What does this teach you?

R.C. Sproul, in commenting on the above passage, says:

> *God frowns upon racists. . . . I don't see anything, even in Scripture, that would prohibit interracial marriage other than the problems people might face in terms of cultural prejudices. Any couple that chooses to get married in a culture that has a high degree of racisim is asking for all kinds of tension directed against their marriage. If they are willing to do that, it doesn't mean that they are sinning by going ahead and entering into a marriage covenant.*[21]

Personal Action Assignment

If you have children or grandchildren (or if you are single yourself), pray through Philippians 1:9-10. Pray for depth of insight concerning a marriage partner.

Day 5: Blessing Your Daughter-in-Law

Once the decision is made, whether or not she is your dream daughter-in-law, you would be wise to bless her. When that future spouse meets you she is hoping for verbal and nonverbal signs that shout your delight! She wants to be loved. She may come with a lack of confidence, fearing she isn't pretty or smart enough. She may come with the tattered baggage of a divorced family. She longs for you to embrace her, no matter what, and she will always remember how you first received her.

Always, but in the early years particularly, she will long to know that you value her. Be generous with compliments on her cooking, her homemaking, her mothering, and her character. Give her the kind of grace and love you would give a daughter and she will become your daughter.

A life-changing classic book is *The Blessing* by Gary Smalley and John Trent. What is the blessing? It is placing *a high value on a person* and demonstrating it through words, touch, gifts, and time. Smalley and Trent say:

> *Without question, one of the greatest gifts parents can give their child is their blessing when it comes to that child's marriage. When parents withhold the blessing from their children for cheating them out of a "high church" wedding, or for marrying a Greek instead of Czech, a German instead of an Italian, or for choosing to attend First Presbyterian rather than Second Baptist, they hit below the belt.*

> *We are not talking about parents who agonize over their believing son who is set on marrying an unbelieving woman or the parents who face the possibility that their never-married daughter may marry a man fresh from his fifth divorce.* Yet even in these situations parents can still demonstrate love for their child in spite of disapproving of his or her actions.[22]

15. What does a mother-in-law stand to gain from being positive and accepting toward her daughter-in-law? What does she stand to lose by being negative?

16. Find all the evidence that you can from Ruth 1 that Naomi loved and blessed her daughters-in-law.

17. If you are married, think back to the efforts you made in the early years as a wife and homemaker. What were some of the specific things you did? What were your feelings? (Pride? Lack of confidence?)

What would a blessing have meant to you? What does it mean to you today?

18. If you are a mother-in-law, what are some ways you could bless your daughter-in-law or son-in-law?

From your hymnal sing, "Make Me a Blessing."

Day 6: Naomi's Prayer for Ruth and Orpah

Despite great famine in her life, Naomi still believed that God was personal and powerful. If He chose, He could bestow blessing. Her prayer is very specific, which shows her faith. (It isn't risky to ask for a general blessing but it shows courage to ask for a husband or a baby!)

However, Naomi probably is thinking: "What Jewish man in Bethlehem would marry a Moabitess?" So she sends them back to find a Moabite man. Her faith goes so far, but then falters.

Also, she will not consider asking them to remain single. It was hard to be single in days when women were considered the property of males! A widow without sons or sons-in-law was in dire straits. Naomi doesn't feel she can ask her daughters to give up the chance of marriage, so better a Moabite man than no man!

Though Naomi's security should have been in God instead of in marriage, we've got to give her latitude. Perhaps if Naomi were not in high tide grief she would have realized that nothing is impossible with God.

19. Some Christian single women today think, "Better a non-Christian or a weak Christian man than no man." What would you tell them?

20. Read Naomi's intercessory prayer in Ruth 1:8-9.
    A. What does Naomi ask God for on behalf of her daughters-in-law?

    B. How does she indirectly praise her daughters-in-law?

    C. How does she describe marriage?

21. The word translated "rest" in Ruth 1:9 is from the Hebrew word *menuchah* and implies security, love, comfort, and blessing. A good marriage should provide a haven from the storms of this world. If you are married, how are you helping to make your home a haven?

How could you make it more of a haven?

22. The word *menuchah* is used in Deuteronomy 28:65-67. What, according to this passage, is the lack of "rest" like?

The above description might sound like Naomi was being overly dramatic in her prayers, yet, in reality, she may not have been. Single women could not own property and farming was the main way of making a living. Orpah and Ruth had left their fathers' homes (and perhaps their fathers were not too pleased about their marriages to Israelite men). Samuel Cox said that Naomi feared they would have a life of servitude, neglect, or license. But a husband could give protection.[23] God had given the Israelites laws to help widows in their distress (Deuteronomy 24:17, 19; 27:19) but it is clear that those laws were often disregarded for the prophets railed against the Israelites for their lack of sympathy toward widows (Jeremiah 7:6; Malachi 3:5).

23. The unfailing love for which Naomi praises her daughters and for which she prays is called in Hebrew, *hesed*. Ruth has been called the book of *hesed*. What do you learn about *hesed* from the following?
    A. Lamentations 3:22-23

    B. Psalm 36:7

In your personal quiet time, turn to "Great Is Thy Faithfulness" in your hymnal and sing it in praise to the Lord. Then ask Him to help you to show that kind of hesed to others.

24. What do you think you will remember from this lesson?

Prayer Time

In the Book of Ruth believers bless one another with prayers. Today, stand in a circle and hold hands. Pray clockwise, having each woman bless the woman on her right with a prayer as simple as: "Lord, please bless Cindy" or, a more specific prayer, such as, "Father, thank You for Cindy's gentle spirit." If you do not want to pray out loud, pray silently, and squeeze the woman's hand to the left of you so that she will know it is her turn.

Three

But Ruth Clung to Her

*I*t's a passionate scene. There must have been shock on their faces when Naomi told them to go back. We know there were tears. They lifted their voices, crying: "We will go back with you to your people" (Ruth 1:10).

But Naomi is adamant, at least on the surface. The Book of Ruth has exquisite poetic refrains. Here there are three iron statements, three heavy chords of despair. But they are followed, if you listen closely, by a faint melody of hope in the form of questions. Murray D. Gowan helps us to see the pattern:

> But Naomi said,
> "RETURN, MY DAUGHTERS!
> Why go with me?
> Are there still sons in my womb?
> that they might become your husbands?
> RETURN, MY DAUGHTERS, GO!
> For I am too old to have a husband.
> For were I to say, 'I have hope,'
> even were I this night to have a husband,
> and, further, were I to bear sons,
> for them would you wait, until they were grown?
> for them would you refrain from having a husband?
> NO, MY DAUGHTERS!
> for my lot is far more bitter than yours,
> for gone out against me is the hand of Yahweh."[24]

Orpah doesn't hear the melody. She hears the cost of following Naomi and Naomi's God and it frightens her. Orpah turns back. Henry Moorhouse, in a little book published in 1881, believes Naomi sent the girls back because she was ashamed that her sons had disobeyed God and married Moabite women. Moorhouse says: "I believe, with all my heart and soul, that Orpah's turning back may be laid at the feet of Naomi."[25] There may be some truth in that, though I don't think Ruth and Orpah would have loved Naomi the way they did if they had sensed a lack of acceptance.

Certainly it was wrong to send them back. But what male commentators might miss here is that women communicate indirectly. Directness can seem demanding and harsh to us. (We may say, "Oh, the trash is so full," rather than, "Please take out the trash now.") A man who said, "Go back," would mean exactly that. A woman might not. A woman might mean, "I want you to come, but I cannot ask so much of you, so perhaps you should go back."

And Orpah must bear part of the responsibility. The choice was hers, even though Naomi didn't encourage her faith. J. Vernon McGee believes that both Orpah and Ruth had become *apparent* followers of Naomi's God, and he bases that on Naomi's statement that Orpah "returned" to her gods.[26] When Orpah discovers there may be a cost in following Naomi's God, she turns back to her people and her gods.

But Ruth clung to her.

Naomi tried again, telling Ruth to go with her sister-in-law, back to her people, back to her gods.

I was moved by a dramatization of this scene by a young woman with Morning Star Ministries who played the part of Naomi, saying: "Ruth fell to her knees and wept like a baby. And she threw her arms around my legs and she cried:

PLEASE DON'T MAKE ME LEAVE YOU.

PLEEEEEASE DON'T MAKE ME LEAVE YOU.

WHERE YOU GO, THERE I WILL GO.

WHERE YOU LIVE, THERE I WILL LIVE."[27]

The "whither thou goest" passage has immortalized Ruth. Many composers have used it for wedding music. Though the vow was spoken by one woman to another, it *is* similar to a wedding vow, and the word "clung," or as the *King James Version* translates it, *"clave* unto her" (Ruth 1:14), is the very same word that is used to describe marriage four times in Scripture:

> *Therefore shall a man leave his father and his mother,*
> *and shall cleave unto his wife:*
> *and they shall be one flesh.*
> *(Genesis 2:24, KJV)*

In Ruth 2:11 this parallel is augmented when Boaz tells Ruth: "I've been told all about what you have done . . . how you *left your father and mother."*

In Walter Trobisch's classic on marriage, *I Married You,* he beautifully explains the threefold command of LEAVING, CLEAVING, and BECOMING ONE FLESH. The Hebrew word *cleaving,* Trobisch explains, has the sense of "to stick to, to paste, to be glued to a person. . . . If you try to separate two pieces of paper which are glued together, you tear them both."[28] Trobisch elaborates:

> *Cleaving means love, but love of a special kind. It is love which has made a decision and which is no longer a groping and seeking love. Love which cleaves is mature love, love which has decided to remain faithful. . . .[29]*

The Scripture uses the concept of cleaving to describe marriage (Ephesians 5:31-32), soulmate friendships (1 Samuel 18:1) and, most importantly, our relationship with God. Ruth, a Moabitess, clung to Naomi's God the way many Israelites were failing to do. Joshua exhorted the Israelites to continue to cleave, to hold fast, to the Lord (Joshua 23:8).

Cleaving. A fascinating concept. There are not many marriages where the couple completely cleaves. (There are not many friendships where the two are faithful for life. There are not many believers who have really died to self, left the old way of life completely behind, and clung to God.)

But, Ruth clung to her.

And if Ruth could do it, so can we.

Prepare Your Heart to Hear
Ask God to give you a heart like Ruth's, a heart that can hear His quiet melody beneath the din of earthly troubles. Ask Him to help you hear Him each day.

Memory Work
Complete Ruth 1:16-17 from the *King James Version*.

> **And Ruth said: "Entreat me not to leave thee, or to return from following after thee: for whither thou goest, I will go; and where thou lodgest, I will lodge: thy people shall be my people, and thy God my God. Where thou diest, will I die, and there will I be buried: the Lord do so to me, and more also, if aught but death part thee and me."**

Warm-Up
Have women comment on what they learn about cleaving from one of these word pictures:

Walter Trobisch: "two pieces of paper glued together"

First Samuel 18:1: "knit" (soul of Jonathan knit to soul of David)

Joshua 23:8: "But you are to hold fast to the Lord your God"

Day 1: Overview
J. Vernon McGee says, "Ruth was willing to undergo the consequences of following Naomi, whatever they might be. This expression of faith on the part of Ruth was acknowledged of God and rewarded by Him later an hundredfold."[30]

Read through the short Book of Ruth in one sitting. As you read this time, look for two things: evidence of Ruth's cleaving to Naomi *and* to Naomi's God; and, evidence of God's blessing to Ruth for her faith in doing so.

1.   What did you see in reading through Ruth this time?

2. What stood out to you from the Introductory notes to this lesson (pp. 38-40)?

Complete your memory work.

Sing "For the Beauty of the Earth" from your hymnal.

Day 2: Like Empty Husks

Avivah Zornberg, who teaches Torah classes in Jerusalem, compares these widows to empty husks. The walking dead.[31] Bereft of husbands, bereft of children, bereft of their ability to own property. Naomi keeps telling us, in different ways, that she is empty. She has empty arms, an empty womb, an empty life. "Don't call me Naomi," she tells the women of Bethlehem. "Why call me Naomi?" (*Naomi* means "sweet or pleasant.") "I went away full, but the Lord has brought me back empty."

Jan Titterington, in a penetrating article in *His,* says:

Frequently a woman's feelings of self-worth are strongly tied to success in the "get your man at all costs" game. When we fail to find a lasting romantic relationship we see ourselves as worthless. As Christians we need to be reminded frequently that our value as human beings is something bestowed on us by God regardless of marital status.

. . . Our hopes for happiness are to be based not on a relationship with the right man, but on Christ and His promise to meet all of our needs, including the need for a husband. Remember Ruth: Like every normal woman she must have desired the esteem, satisfaction and security that accompany marriage and children. Yet she willingly left her familiar homeland, surrendered her rights there and made Naomi's land and people her own. She not only chose to stay with Naomi and dwell in Israel; she embraced the Lord with a faith that might very well shame the children of Israel. And God rewarded that faith.[32]

I have often reflected on Corrie ten Boom's warning not to hold anyone or anything too tightly for we have a loving Father who may pry our fingers away. Women often cling too tightly to people, expecting them to be what only God can be. When a woman attempts suicide, it is often because of a failed relationship. She feels empty and hopeless because she has put her trust, not in God, but in people.

3.   Find the images of emptiness in Ruth 1:11-21.

What do you think was the source of Naomi's identity? Explain.

Men often cling too tightly to power or to money, expecting them to be what only God can be. When a man attempts suicide, it is often because of a failure in a job or a significant financial loss. He feels empty and hopeless because he has put his trust, not in God, but in power or money.

4.   Solomon, Ruth's great great grandson, had everything a person in this world might want. Yet Solomon turned away from God and ran after various things "under the sun." What pursuits does he describe in Ecclesiastes 2:1-10?

What conclusion does he come to in Ecclesiastes 2:11?

And in Ecclesiastes 2:17-18?

5. We can tell whether we are clinging to God or to things under the sun by evaluating our thoughts and priorities.
When you have a free moment, to where or to whom do your thoughts wander?

Are you eager to spend time with God on a daily basis or do other things crowd Him out?

What do you talk about? Is your conversation centered on eternal or transitory things?

Does your checkbook reveal a heart for God?

From your hymnal sing, "As the Deer" and "The Solid Rock."

Day 3: It Is in Dying That We Find Life

At this critical juncture, Orpah and Ruth take opposite paths literally and spiritually. Orpah tries to save herself and Ruth dies to her own desires and puts her trust in Naomi's God.

The most natural response in the world is to try to save yourself. BUT IT IS NOT GOD'S WAY. He tells us to die to ourselves so that we might live.

6.   In Luke 23, Jesus is told to do the same thing three times by people in the world. Find it in verses 35, 37, and 39.

Why didn't He?

7.   In Philippians 2:5-11, we are told to have the same attitude that Jesus did. What was that attitude and how did God bless Him for it?

Notice that Jesus did not "cling" or "grasp" to His life. This is similar to the word for cleave. Orpah held fast to her old safe way of life.

8.   What similar command are we given in 2 Corinthians 5:15?

How do you believe God would have you obey this personally?

9.   Remember the parallel God is constantly making between the land, the harvest, and our lives. Jesus makes a crucial one in John 12:24-25. What is the picture and what does it mean?

How do Ruth and Orpah illustrate the contrast of John 12:24?

10. The person who surrenders her life to God and clings to Him will be filled. The same word *cleave* that is used to describe Ruth's choice to cling to Naomi and Naomi's God is used to describe the relationship God wants us to have with Him. Describe, on the basis of each of these passages, why we are to "cleave" or "hold fast" to God rather than the things of this world.

A. Deuteronomy 10:17-22

B. Deuteronomy 30:19-20

In your quiet time sing "He Is Lord."

Day 4: Listen for the Melody

Ruth heard the melody that Orpah missed, and it made all the difference. Poet Alicia Ostriker imagines Ruth's thoughts:

> *My heart, that has no proper language, appeared to be giving me wordless instructions. Leave the country of your fathers, go with your mother-in-law Naomi. She is a kind woman and comes of decent people. Let her people be your people and her god your god. You are at a border. Walk across it. You will arrive under the wings of the Lord.*
>
> *So I went. It was very strange. Naomi complaining, yet I love her. A bitter old woman, yet I cling to her.*[33]

God's ways are strange. His ways are not our ways. His voice is still and small. It's easy to miss the melody. But it's there.

11. In Ruth 1:11-13, explain the impossible scenario that Naomi paints.

> *Naomi's language, describing hypothetically the improbable event of her marrying a man that very night and eventually bearing sons, is so outrageously exaggerated that it points to a subtext quite different from the point that is ostensibly being made. . . . elaborating on the impossible . . . points to hidden desires and hopes. . . . behind the language of seeming desperation lurks the vision of a potential miracle.*
> *Nehama Aschkenasy*[34]

12. What do you think Naomi truly wanted to happen? (Don't be surprised if you don't agree, because Naomi, like most women, was mysterious. But explore her words, exchange your views, and Naomi may come alive for you.)

13. Listening is an art. Hearing the still small voice of God. Hearing the meaning beneath the words of our loved ones. Drawing out the deep dark waters of another's soul. What do you learn about the art of listening from the following passages?
     A. 1 Kings 19:11-12

     B. Proverbs 1:5

     C. Proverbs 20:5

14. Eight times in the Gospels and eight times in Revelation the Lord says: "He who has ears, let him hear." What are some ways you might better hear the Lord? What are some ways you might better hear what other people are really saying?

15. Take a moment now and write down some of the most important messages God has ever given you through His Word or His Spirit.

Day 5: Tested Hearts

In the Parable of the Sower, Jesus explains how different soils represent different hearts. We often do not know the quality of a soil until time has passed. Some soil may be rocky and thin. Jesus describes that person as one who "hears the word and at once receives it with joy. But since he has no root, he lasts only a short time. When trouble or persecution comes because of the word, he quickly falls away" (Matthew 13:20-21).

Perhaps J. Vernon McGee is right that both Orpah and Ruth, when they married or sometime during the years with Naomi and her sons, had at least taken up some of the traditions and principles of the Jewish faith. But now, their hearts are tested. Are they truly worshipers of the God of Israel or was it just for the sake of family harmony?

16. Naomi lets Orpah and Ruth know there may be a cost if they come with her to Bethlehem. What might that be?

17. For most adults who choose Christ, there is a cost. For some it is very high. What are some possible costs that people have had to consider?

Why might a woman who is living with a man or who is married to an unbeliever hesitate to choose Christ? What advice would you give her?

How does the way we respond to "the cost" reveal the quality of our hearts?

Using Ruth as an example, how does God respond to the person who counts the cost and chooses to continue to follow Christ?

So often, because of our faithless hearts, we want to know God's will before we surrender. We are not willing to trust as Abraham and Ruth did. They followed God not knowing precisely what lay ahead. They trusted God, not because of what He could give them, but because they believed He was God and would do all things well in His time.

I do not think Ruth came to God because she thought He would give her a husband and a baby, though He eventually did, but because she believed He was God and that she, and the idols of Moab, were not.

Those who come to God for other reasons, as Orpah may have initially, will be found out. Their hearts, sooner or later, will be tested.

Review your memory passage.

Day 6: Taste and See That the Lord Is Good

Ruth was able to let go of her old way of life because she had tasted the goodness of the Lord. The Scripture doesn't tell us *just* to die to ourselves and to the things of the world, but to live to God. This is a choice we make at salvation, but it is also an ongoing choice we make every moment of every day.

As we seek God with all of our hearts, spending time in His Word, responding to His Spirit, we will taste and see that He is good! We will discover His eyes are upon us and His ears are open to our prayers just as Ruth discovered. We will discover that He fills up our empty arms, as He did with Ruth and Naomi. We will taste and see that the Lord is good.

18. How might Ruth have tasted God's goodness? (Consider the whole book.)

Read Psalm 34, which was written by Ruth's great grandson, David.

19. Find examples of the Lord's goodness toward the righteous. Give verse references.

20. What are some ways we can die to self and live to God as listed in Psalm 34:13-14?

How do you see Ruth doing the above?

21. Give recent examples from your own life of blessings God has bestowed upon you as you have lived for Him.

22. What do you think you will remember from this lesson?

Prayer Time

Often we pray for blessings but forget to ask God to empower us to live the kind of lives which He blesses. Today, make yourself vulnerable and ask God to help you to die to self and live for Him in a specific way. Then allow one or two sisters to support you audibly. Then another woman should lift up her request. For example:

Lori: "Father, help me to cling to You instead of to food."
Nancy: "Yes, Lord, I agree."
Kristy: "Help Lori taste and see that You are good."
Silence
Kristy: "Father, help me to keep my tongue from evil."
Lori: "I agree, Lord."

Four

Giving Your Mother-in-Law Grace

I have been on both sides now. Over thirty years ago I was the future daughter-in-law, full of insecurity, longing for the blessing. I remember the reserve on the face of my future mother-in-law as I perched nervously on the sofa during our first conversation. She was smiling and pleasant, but I saw fear in her eyes. She was thinking, "Isn't she too young?" (Oh, I was!) "Will she be able to cook?" (Chocolate chip cookies!) "Is she spoiled?" (Yes!)

Did I give her grace for her initial caution? No! I wanted her to do CARTWHEELS around the living room at the prospect of having *me* as a daughter-in-law! Instead, her hands were folded tightly, her voice a bit cool. Instead of giving her a little grace, I harbored resentment for years.

Now I regret that deeply. We lost precious time. When I came to Christ in the second year of our marriage, I began to give her grace, but even then, it was a trickle instead of a flow. How I wish it had flowed from the very beginning.

Philip Yancey says that giving grace is costly. It hurts to forgive someone who has hurt you. That's why we don't want to do it. But Yancey also says, perceptively, that the only thing more costly than giving grace is the alternative.[35] When we refuse to give grace we quench the Spirit of God, hurting ourselves and those close to us.

Now that I have experienced the other side as well, that of being a mother-in-law, I am *much more* compassionate. I understand how every ounce of a mother's heart wants to protect her child from disaster. She remembers how young and foolish she was, so she steps up, like a safety guard at a busy street, and holds out her arms, saying: "Slow down! Look both ways! It's easy to miss things!" (And it is—especially if you are in a hurry!) If her child brings someone home who is from an unhealthy family (and alcoholism, abuse, divorce, etc. are rampant today) the alarms ring.

Some of this is prudent. As parents we have a responsibility to help our children slow down and think clearly, for many have married in haste and repented in leisure. But while we are doing that, we must also be careful not to crush that potential mate. She's scared. It's not her fault if her parents divorced or her daddy had a drinking problem. She needs you to embrace her. She may not be your dream daughter-in-law, but she needs you to love her and to see, through the eyes of faith, her potential. It really isn't fair to ask if she's pretty enough, or Baptist enough, or domestic enough. The only fair question is, "Does she love the Lord with all her heart, soul, and mind?" Because if that is true, God will take care of the rest.

Likewise, daughters-in-law need to learn from Ruth and give their mothers-in-law a little grace. Sometimes daughters-in-law expect their mothers-in-law to have it all together because they cannot imagine that a woman who is *so old* would be anything less than mature. They forget that she is a *person* with insecurities as well. She may be wondering if she can bond with you, fearing she will lose her son. So often the daughter-in-law can't seem to give grace! Go all the way to Bethlehem with her like Ruth did? NO WAY! MAKE HER PAY!

Even a fifty-year-old can stick her foot in her mouth, and I have! The grace that I have received from my daughter-in-law and son-in-law has shamed me, making me wish I had been more gracious to my mother-in-law early on.

Ruth certainly had wisdom beyond her years. If Naomi was less than enthusiastic initially, Ruth forgave her. If the reason that Naomi didn't want to take Ruth and Orpah to Bethlehem did indeed have something to do with her shame in their Moabite nationality, Ruth looks right past that. When Naomi is unpleasant and bitter, Ruth doesn't take it personally. She knows Naomi is hurting, and she determines to restore her.

Orpah doesn't give grace and loses everything.

Ruth gives grace and is rewarded one hundredfold.

Prepare Your Heart to Hear

Sing "Open My Eyes, Lord," from your hymnal, each day, before you study.

Memory Work

Review Ruth 1:16-17 each day. As you do, ask God to show you how this promise has a deeper meaning which involves your relationship to Him.

Warm-Up

Grace can be shown through forgiveness, kindnesses, gifts. Finish this sentence:
   A time when I received grace from someone recently was when

Day 1: Overview

Ruth is the primary agent of grace in this story, but it can also be seen in others. Read through the Book of Ruth and find evidence of grace in the way people treated one another.

1.   What did you find? (Give references.)

2.   What stood out to you from the Introduction to this lesson (pp. 51-52)?

Day 2: Naomi's Honesty in Grief

Naomi's honesty was one of the reasons Ruth understood her. Some have criticized Naomi's negative testimony about God. But if you look closely, she never says God was wrong, she simply says He was severe with her. She grieves honestly. I believe that Naomi's honesty is one of the reasons that Ruth's faith, when tested, proved true.

Some people come to Christ because they have heard that Christ will give them an abundant life. But then, when trials come, they are surprised! They say, "I thought this road was going to be easy! What's going on here? I'm going back to Moab!"

Others, like Ruth, come because they believe God is God and there is no other. Even when the road is hard, they turn to God, because there is no one else to whom they can turn. They have a realistic perspective of the Christian life because someone told them the truth. God is good, but He is also holy and He wants everything! When people were clamoring after Jesus, wanting the good things He could give, He turned around and said: "Estimate the cost" (Luke 14:28).

God hates lies, deceit, and guile. He is pleased when we can be honest with Him and do not cover our sin, doubts, and fears. (After all, He knows them anyway.) He is pleased when we can be honest with *ourselves* through the power of His Holy Spirit. And He doesn't need us to cover for Him to *others*. When we are hurting, we can say so. God is God. He can take care of Himself.

3. Meditate on Naomi's statements about God in the following verses. What does each teach about God and His character?

A. Ruth 1:8-9

B. Ruth 1:13

C. Ruth 1:20-21

4. Naomi's statements could help someone have the fear of God. What are we told about the value of the fear of God in the following?

A. Psalm 34:7-14

B. Psalm 103:11-18

C. Proverbs 1:7

D. Luke 12:5

5.   If God has dealt severely with you because of sin, why might it be good to be honest about this with others?

6.   Some feel that, for the sake of our witness, when we face tragedy, such as the loss of a loved one, that we should not grieve. What do you learn about how God would have us face loss from the following passages?
    A. John 12:32-36

    B. 1 Thessalonians 4:13

In our sorrow over death, we as Christians are sustained by the hope of the resurrection of the dead. But let us not pretend that death does not hurt, and that grief may not be expressed. . . .Let Naomi's tears remind us of the importance of not hiding our feelings. . . . Let Naomi also remind us that our deepest feelings and anxieties are not hidden from God. She deliberately brings her feelings into the open before him. Indeed, she places full responsibility for her plight on God's shoulders! . . . His has been the hand behind the famine and the deaths first of her husband and then of her sons. Yet she holds these bitter experiences in the setting of his covenant promise, by reminding herself and her daughters-in-law of his covenant name: Yahweh, the Lord.
                                                            David Atkinson[36]

7.   We may not understand why God does what He does but, according to Psalm 73:25-28, why must we still return to God?

Review Ruth 1:16-17.

Day 3: Hurting People Hurt People

Instead of withdrawing when Naomi is bitter and complaining, Ruth understands that hurting people hurt people. She doesn't take Naomi's words personally, she hears the faint hope beneath them, and she determines to stand by Naomi's side.

The scene is poignant. After Ruth promises Naomi *everything,* Naomi wounds her, telling the women of Bethlehem she has come back empty! Award-winning author Gloria Golreich writes:

> Her wounds wound Ruth. Naomi is not alone; Ruth is with her. And how can Naomi's heart be empty when Ruth's own heart brims with love for her? But with the wounding comes the balm of forgiveness. Ruth knows (because Naomi has taught her) that in friendship, one must look away, accept small hurts and probe the source of pain. The source of Naomi's pain is her terrible bereavement, her fear of a solitary and poverty-haunted old age. She has, for the moment, forgotten Ruth, but then she is not infallible. Ruth accepts her as she is, as indeed, Naomi has always accepted Ruth.[37]

Read Ruth 1:16-22 carefully.

8. Instead of throwing her arms around Ruth and saying, "Thank God for a friend like you in my time of need," Naomi is silent. How does Ruth 1:18 say she responds?

Why do you think Naomi fails to respond enthusiastically to Ruth's commitment?

9.   Now Naomi and Ruth arrive in Bethlehem. Put yourself in Naomi's shoes. What kind of memories do you think came to her mind as she surveyed her home?

When Naomi returns to the land of Judah, she is suddenly flooded with memories: Elimelech, with his easy laugh . . . Mahlon and Chilion . . . Scenes she thought she had forgotten, vivid with color and feeling, sweep over her. . . . She is blinded by grief.
                              Rabbi Ruth H. Sohn[38]

10. Why do you think the women of Bethlehem are confused about Naomi's identity?

So changed in her appearance, so downcast is she, that they hardly recognize her. As the Midrash puts it, in the old days she was carried by servants on litters, wore cloaks of fine wool, looked hearty and well fed. Now she appears barefoot, dressed in rags, pale and emaciated. And the women said: "Is this Naomi?"
                         Dr. Lois Dubin of Smith College[39]

11. Why do you think Naomi is eager to express her pain to this particular audience?

Why is it therapeutic to express the pain and the details of a loss?

12. What happens to the believer who has trouble being honest about her own spiritual struggles to trusted friends and pretends all is well or only asks for prayer for others?

Review your memory work.

Day 4: Ruth's Response

There are very few fifty-year friendships. Even when God blesses us with a soul mate, we have trouble being true to her for life. Research shows that while many soul mates can pass the tests of distance and stress, they have trouble passing the test of hurt feelings. When we feel betrayed, we withdraw.

One woman said: "A good warm friendship is like a good warm fire. It needs continual stoking."[40] But when we get our feelings hurt, we tend to lay the poker down. And the fire dies.

Ruth is remarkable. She keeps stoking the fire that burned her. Most women would have turned back to Moab, but Ruth is steadfast in her love. She has the kind of faith that keeps her from giving up, even in the face of rejection. She somehow, beneath Naomi's laments, hears the still small voice of God whispering: "Don't give up. Love the way I have loved you. In due time you will reap a harvest if you do not give up."

13. How did Ruth pass the tests of stress and distance in her friendship to Naomi?

14. List the promises Ruth made to Naomi in Ruth 1:16-17.

In light of what she had seen in Naomi's life, comment on verse 17b.

15. Complete the following, realizing there may be repetition and more than one principle in each case.

Grace Chart

	RUTH'S ACTION	GRACE PRINCIPLE	PERSONAL APPLICATION
Ruth 1:22			
Ruth 2:2-3			
Ruth 2:17-18			
Ruth 2:22-23			
Ruth 3:5-6			
Ruth 3:16-17			
Ruth 4:13-17			

16.   Is there anyone in your life whom you have not forgiven? How could you follow Ruth's model and not only forgive, but give unfailing love?

Day 5: Grace, Grace, God's Grace
As God has given grace, so should we.

17.   Complete the following, realizing there may be repetition and more than one principle in each case.

Grace Chart

	GOD'S ACTION	GRACE PRINCIPLE	PERSONAL APPLICATION
John 3:16			
Romans 5:8			
Psalm 145:8			
Jeremiah 29:11			

Day 6: Mothers-in-Law
Cartoonists, marriage counselors, and even Scripture (see Micah 7:6 and Matthew 10:35) confirm that relationships with mothers-in-law are often troubled. Marriage counselor Walter Trobisch says: "In America and Europe it is usually the mother of the husband who interferes. She just can't believe that this young girl whom he married is able to take care of her precious son. Will she be able to wash his shirts right? Will she know how much salt he likes in his soup?"[41]
     Mothers-in-law make mistakes, and daughters-in-law can have trouble

seeing them as people who need grace. In an essay entitled, "I didn't see that you were Naomi," playwright Merle Field shows a depth of compassion as a daughter-in-law:

> *Wednesday, Thanksgiving weekend, 1971. They are visiting us in our own home for the first time. She walks through the house, past the burlap living-room curtains I have made myself, the bed with a colorful throw which serves as our couch, the bricks-and-board coffee table . . . through to the cheerful yellow kitchen with its ruffled yellow curtains. "The landlord couldn't give you a new sink?"*
>
> *She didn't mean to be unkind. She couldn't see that what I needed was a compliment. She was uncomfortable with compliments. She had been raised to recoil from them. . . . Once, early on, after an unpleasant exchange, I try to "talk" with her. Honestly. About our feelings. She will have none of it.*
>
> *. . . Over the years I learned to have a relationship with her on her terms, first cordial, then friendly, then caring, then loving. Loving without touching, a first for me. We built a relationship on the things we shared—our respect for hard work, our frugal natures, our love of things Jewish, our love of her son, our love of my children.*[42]

18. In the above essay, how do you see Merle giving her mother-in-law grace?

   If you are a mother-in-law, how have your sons-in-law or daughters-in-law given you grace?

19. Why do you think this relationship is often fragile?

   What does a daughter-in-law have to lose by not giving her mother-in-law grace?

Prayer Time

Pair in twos and pray for someone in your life who needs grace from you. Pray God will give you compassion. Pray for God's richest blessing on her (or him).

TO THE FAITHFUL HE SHOWS HIMSELF FAITHFUL

So she went out and began to glean
in the fields behind the harvesters.
As it turned out, she found herself working
in a field belonging to Boaz, who was
from the clan of Elimelech.
—Ruth 2:3

Five

Under His Wings

What a love story! Boaz, a godly, virile, and wealthy man, is mesmerized by Ruth, a destitute but lovely young widow. Are there obstacles? Of course! But is God mighty to overcome those obstacles? You *know* He is, especially for those who fear Him, who have come "under the shadow of His wings."

I have a dear friend whose story parallels Ruth's in many ways. Knowing and loving Jill has brought the story of Ruth alive for me in a contemporary setting. I first met Jill twelve years ago when she and her husband Russ were at a track meet. The picture vivid in my memory is of Russ Wolford that day. A big handsome farmer, Russ had four-year-old Geri perched high upon his shoulders as he led the family in cheers for Gina who was leading in the one-hundred-yard dash. The five on the sidelines screamed and whooped, and then embraced in a jubilant heap when Gina was first over the finish line. All who watched this loving family were warmed.

No one expected that tragedy lurked around the corner.

A year later Russ Wolford was electrocuted in a farming accident.

I visited Jill out at the Wolford farm in her dark days of grief. She was too thin, and her smile, though brave, quivered. She told me she wanted to hold onto the farm for the children's sake, but how? She said the children weren't sleeping: they had nightmares about the accident, of their dad's still body. I wept with her. Together we prayed to God, under whose wings she and the children had taken refuge.

Jill played a song for me that the children had been listening to over and over again on their little tape recorder. It was the only song that seemed to calm them and help them fall asleep. Taken from the word pictures in the Book of Ruth (Ruth 2:12 and 3:9), it is written by Andrew Culverwell:

His Presence

Cover Me
Cover me, Lord, with Your presence,
Cover me, Lord, with Your righteousness,
Cover me, Lord, with Your holiness,
Lord Jesus, cover me.

Under Your shadow, I won't be afraid
Cover me, Lord, til the storm goes away
And then in the heat of a beautiful day,
Lord Jesus, cover me.

Unable to operate the farm, Jill reluctantly rented it out and moved the family to town. But, like Ruth, she trusted God.

Still young, still beautiful, Jill was cautious when men began to inquire concerning her availability. She wanted only God's choice. Years passed.

I stopped to visit Jill one Christmas and she was radiant. With a shy smile, she said: "Dee, I've met someone."

"Tell me everything!" (I was sounding like Naomi in Ruth 3:16.)

And with detail that cannot fit in a Bible study guide, she told me all about Keith Johnson, a godly man, a farmer, who had been through his own personal grief, but was now obviously winning her heart.

I remember their wedding day, a scene reminiscent of the wedding day of Ruth and Boaz. The people of God, who loved them so, rejoiced that the time of sadness was over! We knew challenges lay ahead, but we had seen God's hand in their romance and now we prayed in faith, much as the people of Bethlehem prayed for Ruth and Boaz on their wedding day. Jill, Keith, and the four children stood in a circle at the front of the church, arms intertwined, heads bowed, as the body of Christ prayed for their new family.

Boaz bought back the farm that belonged to Ruth's late husband, brother-in-law, and father-in-law. He raised up their first son in the late family's name. He embraced Naomi as part of the family. It takes a godly man to do those things.

Keith sold his own property in order to redeem Jill's rented farm and to purchase additional adjoining acreage that belonged to Jill's brother-in-law, Roger Wolford. The family moved back to their farm where Keith erected a sign: "The Wolford-Johnsons." The Wolford name has not been blotted out. In addition, Keith has embraced the extended family. As Boaz brought Naomi into his home, Keith has kept the children in close contact with Russ' parents. It takes a godly man to do those things.

Every time I drive by the "Wolford-Johnsons," I think of Ruth and Boaz, and of our God, who is eager to give refuge to those of noble character, and who sees to it that the name of the righteous is not blotted out.

Prepare Your Heart to Hear
Pray each day that the Lord, the God of Israel, under whose wings you have come to take refuge, will give you insight.

Memory Work
Over the next three weeks you will memorize Ruth 2:10-12. This week learn:

At this, she bowed down with her face to the ground. She exclaimed, "Why have I found such favor in your eyes that you notice me—a foreigner?"

Warm-Up
In one breath, have a few tell about one of their favorite love stories (book, movie, personal).

Day 1: Overview
G. Campbell Morgan says that the lives of Ruth and Boaz illustrate saintship. Ruth trusted God amidst desperate circumstances. She and Boaz lived godly lives in the degenerate days of the judges. Morgan describes the character of each:

Ruth was a woman capable of love, characterized by modesty, of fine gentleness, of splendid courage; a woman in all the grace and beauty of womanhood. Boaz was a man of integrity, of courtesy, of tender passion, of courage; a man in all the strength and glory of manhood.[43]

1.   Read through Ruth 2 and watch the building romance. What do you see that you have not seen before?

2.   What stood out to you from the Introduction to this lesson?(pp. 63–65)

Begin memorizing Ruth 2:10.

Day 2: The Barley Harvest Was Beginning

The first chapter of Ruth, a chapter of famine and death, closes with a melody of hope. Two widows arrive "in Bethlehem as the barley harvest was beginning" (Ruth 1:22). God is providing for His people again, and the fields are full of hundreds of enthusiastic reapers and gleaners. Samuel Cox paints the scene:

> *The field is thick with waving barley. The reapers cut their way into it with sickles. . . . Behind them the women gather up the armfuls and bind them into sheaves. Still further in the rear follow the widow and stranger, who, according to the Hebrew law, have the right to glean after the reapers. . . . (Skins filled with water hang from the branch of a nearby tree, kept cool by the soft breeze. A house is also there in which those who are weary may rest from the glare and heat of the sun.)*[44]

3.   Chapter 2 opens when the "barley harvest was beginning." How does it close?

Do you see any parallel with the theme of restoration?

4.   Ruth 2:1 gives us a clue as to whom the agent of restoration will be. Who is he and what do you learn about him?

5.   When we are told Boaz was from the clan of Elimelech, the faint melody of Ruth 1 grows stronger. When you were from the same clan, you were considered "a brother." What do we learn about a brother's responsibility in Deuteronomy 25:5-10?

6.   In Ruth 2:2, Ruth shows knowledge of another levitical law found in Deuteronomy 24:19-22. What does it say?

What reason does God give in Deuteronomy 24:19 for being kind to the less fortunate?

What reason does He give in Deuteronomy 24:22 for being kind? What do you think He means by this?

7.   Scripture often tells us that we are to love others as we have been loved by God. Explain how you see this in:
     A. 2 Corinthians 5:18-20

     B. Ephesians 5:32

     C. 1 John 3:16-17

8. We become more compassionate when we remember what it was like to be hurting. God wants the Israelites to remember their years in slavery and as strangers in a foreign land. If possible, recall your pain when you were:
    A. Going through adolescence

    B. In darkness, in slavery to sin

    C. New in town

9. What does 2 Corinthians 1:3-4 teach?

    Through what kinds of troubles has God brought you so that you are now equipped to bring comfort to others?

10. Is God speaking to you in some way to be more compassionate to someone who is in one of the above situations? If so, what action will you take?

From your hymnal sing "And Can It Be?"

Day 3: Introducing Boaz, a Mighty Man of Wealth

Godly men are incredibly attractive. As a married woman (and a very happily married woman who wants to stay happily married to her WONDERFUL and VERY GODLY husband) if there is a man I must guard my emotions against, it is a godly man. There is a richness, a depth, a largeness of character in godly men that dwarfs the spiritually anemic.

Boaz was such a man! Robert A. Watson says: "From the moment he appears in the narrative we note in him a certain largeness of character."[45]

Some have thought that Boaz was an old man because of his words in Ruth 3:10 when he blesses Ruth for not running after the younger men. But this doesn't mean that Boaz was old. J. Vernon McGee says: "The normal inference from this passage is that Boaz was not a boy but a man of middle age. Quite evidently, he was in the full vigor of manhood. . . ."[46]

Both poverty and wealth test character. Boaz passed the test of wealth. He ate with his servants, he remembered the poor, and was ever mindful of the Lord.

What a guy!

Review your memory work.

Read Ruth 2:3-5.

11.   As Ruth goes out and chooses from all the fields in Bethlehem, in whose field does she "happen"?

What fact does the author of Ruth repeat about Boaz in verse 3? Why do you think this fact is repeated?

12.   Describe the kind of man that Boaz seems to be in our first glimpse of him in verse 4.

There is no separation between the "sacred" and the "secular": the whole of life is lived as "before the face of God." Here we have what A. Maclaren calls the "lovely little picture of a harvest field, where passers-by shout their good wishes to the glad toilers, and are answered by these with like salutations. 'The blessing of the Lord be upon you! We bless you in the name of the Lord!'"[47]

13. How might verse 5 demonstrate an immediate answer to prayer?

What are the prayers called out in verse 4?

14. What does Boaz's question reveal about the culture?

Read Ruth 2:6-9.

15. What does Boaz learn about Ruth's character from his foreman?

16. Look at each sentence Boaz speaks to Ruth in 2:8-9 and explain how he understood and met her fears and needs.

17. Boaz's greeting demonstrates a robust and thankful spirit. Thankful spirits are often generous. Why do you think that is?

18. What are your impressions of Boaz at this point? Why?

Day 4: Glimmering beneath the Figure of Boaz Is Christ

Hidden in every book in the Old Testament is Jesus, for the Old Testament is the drumbeat for the entrance of Christ in the New Testament. In the Book of Ruth, Christ is hidden in the figure of Boaz. This will become increasingly clear in Ruth 3, when Boaz becomes the "kinsman-redeemer."

19. How can you see Christ in the figure of Boaz in Ruth 2:8-9?

How has Christ provided for you or protected you recently?

20. How does Ruth respond to Boaz in Ruth 2:10?

Read 2 Samuel 9.

There is a beautiful parallel here. Ruth's great grandson, David, treats the crippled Mephibosheth with kindness that resembles that of Boaz toward Ruth. In biblical days, handicapped people were not valued. Also, family members of the last king were often executed, so that there would be no threat to the new king. This helps us to understand why Mephibosheth, when called before the king, is so afraid.

21. Compare Ruth 2:8-10 and 2 Samuel 9. Find similarities in the attitude, posture, and words of Ruth and Mephibosheth.

22. Look briefly ahead to Ruth 3:11 and compare it to 2 Samuel 9:7. What similarity do you see?

23. Compare both of these scenes to the scene in Isaiah 6:1-7 in which Isaiah saw the Lord. What similarities do you see?

24. When you see the Lord face-to-face, how do you think you will feel? What do you think He will say to you?

**Spend some time in praise to the Lord, using your hymnal.
Good choices would be "I Will Sing of My Redeemer" and "Under His Wings."**

Day 5: Love Is a Many Splendored Thing

What makes romance *especially* exciting? The hand of God! Surely the author of Ruth wants us to know that this is not a chance meeting. Out of all the fields of Bethlehem, "as it turned out," Ruth finds herself in the field of Boaz. And "just then" Boaz arrives. He notices her and tells her why.

Read Ruth 2:10-17.

25. What has impressed Boaz about Ruth?

How does he show her that he understands the difficulty of what she has done?

How does he pray for her?

Some have said that Boaz is shirking his responsibility here. (James 2:15-16 says that if we are equipped to help we shouldn't just pray God will help the destitute.) However, Boaz does help Ruth, although he does not propose marriage according to the Mosaic Law. Perhaps he is unsure of her interest. Perhaps he is aware of the nearer kinsman who should be given the first right to propose.

26. The word picture that Boaz gives is a theme in Scripture. What else do you learn about the character of God from:
    A. Psalm 17:8

B. Psalm 36:7

C. Psalm 57:1

D. Psalm 63:7

27. How does Boaz continue to show kindness to Ruth in 2:14?

28. Based on this account, what advice would you give to a woman who hopes to attract a godly man?

Day 6: Restoration Begins for Naomi

It's a heartwarming scene. Ruth has been determined to fill the empty arms of her mother-in-law. Now she comes home carrying a huge bag of freshly threshed grain. Naomi, amazed, asks who has been so kind to Ruth. Cyril Barber says that "the innocent way in which Ruth mentions Boaz's name shows she has no idea of the dramatic import of her words."[48]

Read Ruth 2:17-23.

29. The grain was so plentiful, Ruth had to thresh it. Even threshed, it amounted to 3/5 of a bushel.
     A. Describe Ruth's work habits (verses 17–18).

B. Describe Ruth's eating habits (verse 18).

In studying thin people, I learned that they do four fundamental things that fat people don't.
1. *They hardly ever eat unless their body is hungry.*
2. *They eat exactly what they want to eat.*
3. *They don't eat unconsciously; they stay conscious of what they are eating and the effect it's having on their body.*
4. *They stop eating when their body's hunger goes away.*

Dr. Bob Schwartz, *Diets Don't Work!*[49]

30. Notice the escalating excitement between Naomi and Ruth:
    A. How can you see initial excitement in Naomi in verse 19?

    B. How does Ruth's innocent reply escalate Naomi's excitement? (verses 19–20)

    C. How does Ruth now add to the excitement? (verse 21)

    D. How does Naomi change from apathy to action? (verse 22)

Like gently moving streams, Ruth and Naomi join together, giving one another a fresh water supply and the energy to enter the rushing, exciting river of God.

31. Think about a time when you and another sister (or sisters) in Christ helped each other ride the exciting rapids of God's will. Share. (And in the sharing, you

will be escalating the group's excitement in the wonder of being children of God.)

32. Ruth provides a model for restoring the brokenhearted. The following Scriptures give advice on this subject. Explain first what they tell us to do (or not to do) if we are going to restore another. Then explain how Ruth did it right!
    A. Proverbs 20:6

    B. Proverbs 25:20

    C. Romans 12:12-14

    D. Galatians 6:9-10

    E. 1 Peter 4:8

Review your memory passage.

33. What has God impressed on your heart from this entire lesson?

Prayer Time
In conversational prayer, lift up your own need (or an impression described in question 33) and allow two or three other women to say sentence prayers for you. When there is a pause, another woman should lift up her need. Close with "God Is So Good" or another familiar chorus.

Six

My Daughter, Should I Not Try to Find a Home for You?

 aomi, numbed by grief, has awakened. Ruth, through her steadfast kindnesses and faith, has brought restoration to Naomi.

Now Naomi is going to see to the redeeming of Ruth.

How good of God to give us this beautiful portrait of the power, the value, and the sheer beauty of women's friendships.

All of my life, women have ministered to me through friendship. Women are like roses: breathtakingly beautiful, created to open petal after petal of fragrant loveliness in a world often devoid of softness and beauty. Yes, we have thorns, but the beauty of the rose more than compensates for the occasional jab of a thorn.

After one conference where I spoke about women's friendships a woman stood during the sharing time and said:

We're always being told that women are catty, gossipy, and shallow. It was so good to hear about the beauty of women's friendships. It strikes a true chord in my heart, one I have needed to hear. As sisters in Christ, we and our friendships have worth in God's eyes.

I am absolutely convinced that God gave us this book, in part, to affirm us as women of our value and of our value to one another.

Prepare Your Heart to Hear

To the faithful, God shows Himself faithful. Each day, run to the Lord, treating Him like the lover He longs to be to you.

Memory Work
Complete Ruth 2:10-12.

> At this, she bowed down with her face to the ground. She exclaimed, "Why have I found such favor in your eyes that you notice me—a foreigner?"
>
> Boaz replied, "I've been told all about what you have done for your mother-in-law since the death of your husband— how you left your father and mother and your homeland and came to live with a people you did not know before.
>
> May the Lord repay you for what you have done. May you be richly rewarded by the Lord, the God of Israel, under whose wings you have come to take refuge."

Warm-Up
Go around the circle clockwise, having each woman share one reason she is thankful for the woman on her right.

Day 1: Overview
As you read Ruth 3, see how active Naomi is in helping Ruth, how respectful Ruth is of Naomi, and how intimately they share. This is friendship at its best.

1.   Read Ruth 3 and ask God to show you something new about moving to a deeper level in friendship. What did you see?

2.   What stood out to you from the Introduction? (p. 76)

Sing "Blest Be the Tie That Binds" from your hymnal.

Spend five minutes on your memory passage.

Day 2: Matchmaker, Matchmaker!

Perhaps it is not fair to call it matchmaking, for God led Ruth into the field of Boaz and Boaz certainly showed an interest in Ruth. However, Naomi is aware that Ruth has been in Boaz's field for six weeks and there has been no proposal. Perhaps the man needs a little encouragement!

Naomi came up with a bold plan. And despite the seeming audacity of it, despite the risk of danger or embarrassment, Ruth follows Naomi's plan to the letter.

Was Naomi's plan pleasing to God? Or did she go too far?

I agree with Elisabeth Elliot that the man should be the pursuer in a relationship. However, once he has shown an interest, may a woman acknowledge her interest? I think, if it is not overdone (for a godly man will be rightly repulsed by a pursuing woman), but done in a spirit of gentleness, it can be an act of kindness.

But is it overdoing it to call him, stop by his apartment, or go into where he is sleeping at night?

Usually, absolutely. However, we do not live under the Mosaic Law (Deuteronomy 5:5-10). J. Vernon McGee explains that after Boaz had shown an interest in Ruth, according to the Mosaic system, it was incumbent upon Ruth to make a definite move. If she didn't, it would have constituted a rejection of Boaz as a suitor. When Ruth pulled the end of the long mantle that was covering Boaz over herself, she was letting him know she wanted his shelter and protection. "This was a symbolic and modest way of telling Boaz that she would be willing to accept him as the *'goel'* to take Mahlon's place in a leviritic marriage."[50]

Ruth could have gone before the city elders and demanded her rights, but Naomi wisely suggests this discreet act of kindness instead. And this is exactly how Boaz interprets it. If he refuses Ruth, no one needs to know. But he won't. Naomi discerns he is drawn to Ruth. Women have intuition about these things.

Read Ruth 3:1-6.

3. How does Naomi's preface to her plan show her tenderness and concern for Ruth? (verses 1-2)

What can you learn from this concerning friendly persuasion? Concerning mentoring?

4.   Exactly what were Naomi's instructions to Ruth? (3:3-4)

After oxen had tramped out the grain, men threw it into the air with a fork against the night wind. The chaff would be blown away and the good grain would fall to the ground. It was the climax of the harvest and had the spirit of a religious festival. Families enjoyed bonfires, food, and festivity. Ruth could be lost in the crowd. After the people went home, a few men slept there to guard the grain against robbers. (Remember Ruth took place in the days of the Judges, so guards were needed.)

5.   Put yourself in Ruth's place. What fears might she have had?

6.   Share a time when you stepped out in faith despite the risk of failure. Why did you do it and what happened? (Be brief!)

Sing "I Know Whom I Have Believed" from your hymnal.

Day 3: I Will Do Whatever You Say

Most friends are like "annuals," flowers which bless us for a season, but then they fade away. But, now and then, God gives us a perennial, a friend who is there season after season. A soul mate. Someone to whom your soul is knit. And though that friendship may be battered by distance, stress, and misunderstandings, still, there she is, even after the storms of winter have passed.

I have asked God to help me recognize the perennials in my life so that I can be true. Ten years ago, when I was writing *The Friendships of Women,* I prayed about this and God impressed on my heart the names of four long-distance friends to whom I am endeavoring to be true. I want to be there when they need me, no matter the cost, as Ruth was for Naomi.

Lorinda is a perennial in my life. When I was a baby Christian, she befriended me, mentored me, and helped me grow. Immeasurably grateful, I tried to give her a silver tea set that had belonged to my great grandmother. She said, "Dee, I can't possibly take a family heirloom from you!"

I said, "Lorinda, I don't use it. I don't like to polish silver. You have meant so much to me. Your gift is hospitality and I know you would use it. I want to give you a gift of great worth because you are of great worth to me."

Finally Lorinda agreed. Twenty-five years have passed and Lorinda and I have stayed close, despite living 2,000 miles apart, despite stress, despite one major misunderstanding. The silver set has sat, shining, on the center of her formal dining table, and has poured tea for missionaries, college presidents, and women friends.

This summer our daughter Sally was married, and most of my perennials flew out for the wedding. Lorinda was not there because she was in the hospital fighting an aggressive cancer.

But when Sally opened her wedding gift from Lorinda, it was the tea set, along with a letter I will cherish forever.

This is the beauty of women's friendships.

Personal Action Assignment

Ask God to show you the perennials in your life. Some good questions to consider are:

Is my soul knit to hers?
Is her soul knit to mine?
How are you leading, Lord?

To whom is God leading you to be steadfast and true?

7. How does Ruth respond to Naomi's risky plan? (Ruth 3:5)

Read 1 Samuel 20:1-4.

8. What disagreement do soul mates David and Jonathan have?

9. Though David has not articulated it, Jonathan senses David wants him to take on the risky task of finding out if his father has murderous plans. How does Jonathan respond?

How is this similar to Ruth's response in Ruth 3:5?

What does this teach you about soul mate friendships?

10. Think about the story of Lorinda, a perennial friend. Comment on annual and perennial friends. What is the value of each?

Sing "For the Beauty of the Earth" from your hymnal, reflecting particularly on the third verse.

Review your memory work.

Day 4: The Threshing Floor

Naomi was confident that Boaz would behave himself with morality and integrity, and she was right. Some think that because Ruth spent the night that Ruth and Boaz had sexual intercourse. They did not. Cyril Barber explains: "The Hebrew word *lun*, 'to pass the night,' has latent within it the passage of time and does not concern itself with the manner in which the time was spent. If Boaz and Ruth had engaged in sexual relations on the threshing floor then *sakab*, 'to lie (together), to sleep (together)' would have been used. *Lun* is a word devoid of sexual connotations."[51]

Read Ruth 3:6-15.

11. Describe Ruth's actions and words in Ruth 3:7-9.

12. Describe the response of Boaz in each of the following and show how his response shows kindness, integrity, or character:
  A. Verse 10

  B. Verse 11

  C. Verses 12-13

  D. Verse 14

  E. Verse 15

13. What impresses you the most about Boaz from the above? Why?

The customs leading to marriage were different in Ruth's day. Parents arranged marriages, though children sometimes influenced their parents. (See Samson with his parents in Judges 14.) And Boaz's words to Ruth ("You have not run after the younger men") implies that even then young people may have been successful in ignoring the counsel of their parents. Naomi was taking the role of arranging this marriage and Ruth was obeying.

Today Christian parents in the Western world do not arrange marriages, but some ask their children simply to be friends with the opposite sex until they are ready for marriage. Then they recommend the practice of courtship under their guidance. A nineteenth-century Webster's dictionary defines courtship as "the act of wooing in love; solicitation of a woman to marriage."

14. Do you see any principles in this account that could apply to finding a good marriage partner? If so, what?

In our culture, dating can begin in the early teens. Do you see any danger in this? If so, explain.

Some Christian young people are choosing to be friends with the opposite sex but not to engage in dating until they are ready to take on the commitment of marriage. Often they look strongly to their parents for their counsel. Comment.

Day 5: Cover Me, Cover Me

I was twenty-one before I realized who Jesus was. When I knelt to surrender my life to Him, I suddenly became acutely aware of the holiness of God and my own profound wretchedness.

Again and again in Scripture, when people get a glimpse of who Christ really is, they realize how destitute they are, how in need of cleansing and covering. They cannot bear to stand before the Lord naked. Peter cried, "Depart from me, for I am a sinful man, O Lord!" (Luke 5:8) Isaiah said, "Woe is me, I am a man of unclean lips" (Isaiah 6:5). And here Ruth asks Boaz, our Christ-figure, "to cover her." When we see ourselves as we really are, we plead: "Cover me, cover me!"

The Old Testament prophets give us vivid word pictures to show us our need for cleansing and covering.

Prepare your heart by singing "There Is Power in the Blood" from your hymnal. Thank God for His "wonder-working power!"

15. What word picture does Isaiah 1:18 give?

16. In Ezekiel 16:1-14:
    A. How are God's people pictured? (verses 1-5)

    B. How did God respond to their destitute state? (verses 6-7)

    C. What word picture is given in verse 8? What similarity do you see with Ruth 3:9?

    D. What word picture is given in Ezekiel 16:9? What similarity do you see with Ruth 3:3?

    E. What impresses you personally about this picture?

17. Boaz drew Ruth to himself, yet Ruth had to ask Boaz to cover her. How is this a picture of salvation?

18. Have you asked Jesus to cleanse you and cover you with His righteousness? If so, share what happened in a sentence.

Personal Action Assignment
Not only in salvation, but on a daily basis we need the cleansing and covering of our Redeemer. Be still before the Lord. Confess and turn from any sin. Pray through 1 John 1:9.

Day 6: "How Did It Go, My Daughter?"

One of the ways we raise an acquaintance to a friend is by sharing a confidence. When Naomi asks Ruth about her night, Ruth tells her *everything*. (How many daughters-in-law do that?) Each of these women are seeking the other's best. They have therefore learned to trust each other.

Then Naomi encourages Ruth, being confident Boaz will do the right thing, and that the matter will be settled. Naomi, who is restored, is back in her role as a mentor, confidante, and encourager.

Review your memory work.

Read Ruth 3:14-18.

19. How have Ruth's actions escalated her relationship with Boaz to a deeper level of intimacy? What parallel can you see with Christ?

20. How do you see intimacy demonstrated between Ruth and Naomi upon Ruth's return?

If you have a mother-in-law, how willing are you to raise her to a new level of intimacy? If not, is it because of pride or a lack of forgiveness toward past hurts?

21. What wise advice does Naomi give to Ruth?

Sometimes we take action before we have waited upon the Lord. Why is this foolish? Is there an application to your life?

22. Where are you struggling in your walk with God? Would you be willing to share this with a trusted friend?

Prayer Time

An essential for effective prayer is honesty. Vulnerably lift up your own walk with the Lord in group prayer. Pray for each other. Then, wait, for God responds to the honest handmaiden.

Seven

Your Daughter-in-Law Is Better to You Than Seven Sons

The women of Bethlehem tell Naomi that Ruth is better to her than seven sons! Perhaps they remember that when Naomi returned to Bethlehem with Ruth, she said: "I've come back empty."

Naomi was not empty. Ruth has been an amazing gift. Now, the friends are at the home during the birth of Naomi's grandson. Intriguingly, they name the baby! They name him "Obed," which means "servant" and in Ruth 4:14-15, the women say:

Praise be to the Lord, who this day has not left you without a kinsman-redeemer. May he become famous throughout Israel. He will renew your life and sustain you in your old age. For your daughter-in-law, who loves you and who is better to you than seven sons, has given him birth.

Better than seven sons! What an accolade! A perfect family in Israel was seven sons. In cultures where men are valued more than women, rich more than poor, God looks on the heart. And to the faithful He shows Himself faithful.

Prepare Your Heart to Hear
Be faithful in spending quality time with God each day. To the faithful He shows Himself faithful (2 Samuel 22:26).

Memory Work
Complete Ruth 2:10-12.

> **At this, she bowed down with her face to the ground. She exclaimed, "Why have I found such favor in your eyes that you notice me—a foreigner?"**

Boaz replied, "I've been told all about what you have done for your mother-in-law since the death of your husband—how you left your father and mother and your homeland and came to live with a people you did not know before.

"May the Lord repay you for what you have done. May you be richly rewarded by the Lord, the God of Israel, under whose wings you have come to take refuge."

Warm-Up

In groups of three, share an embarrassing moment from a date or wedding. In the large group, ask for nominations for the best.

Day 1: Overview

Our God is alive. He rewards those who diligently seek Him. Therefore, when His children are walking in unbroken fellowship with Him, they can intercede powerfully in prayer for one another. This is the power of the blessing. "Blessing" in the Hebrew comes from a word meaning "to bow the knee." These believers continually "bow their knee" to God and call upon His power to bless one another.

1. Fill in the following chart.

Ruth Blessing Chart

RUTH	BLESSING REQUESTED	RESPONSE FROM GOD
1:8-9		
2:4		
2:12		
2:19		
3:10		
4:11-12		
4:14		

2.   What do you learn from the above exercise?

Complete your memory work.

Day 2: If God Is in a Relationship, He Will Hold It Together

Manipulation is the reverse of faith. If God is real and personal, then we don't need to manipulate. We do what God leads us to do and no more. Then we wait and trust that God will do what is best for us or our children.

God led the women in this book to make their desires known to Boaz. Now there is an obstacle. What is Naomi's advice? "Wait, my daughter." Faith calls for patience. We would be wise to be wary when we are pressured by others to make a decision quickly.

Naomi, Ruth, and Boaz do not panic. There seems to be a quiet confidence that if God is in this relationship, He will hold it together. If not, then God has another plan, and God's ways are always best.

Read Ruth 3:10-13.

3.   The words of Boaz to Ruth show again and again that Boaz believes God will be good to the faithful.
   A. How has Boaz seen faith and character in Ruth? (verses 10-11)

   B. What does Boaz say to Ruth about the nearer kinsman? (verses 12-13)

   C. Why do you think Boaz is offering Ruth to the nearer kinsman? Why do you think he doesn't seem anxious?

Read Ruth 3:14-18.

4.   What advice does Naomi give to Ruth?

5.   Define *manipulation* using a dictionary.

When does a mother cross the line from guidance into manipulation with her children?

6.   As you examine your own heart, are you trying to manipulate anyone? What approach would be more pleasing to God?

Day 3: But Don't Be Foolish

While we should not manipulate, should not try to deceive people, or be God to them, neither should we be foolish. Jesus tells us to be as wise as serpents and as gentle as doves.

Repeatedly in Scripture we have the model of believers approaching difficult people and situations prayerfully and diplomatically. Here Boaz models a wise approach.

The law provided for the poor (Leviticus 25:23-28) and the childless widow (Deuteronomy 25:5-10). Both Boaz and the nearer kinsman were relatives, though they had not been living with Elimelech. However, in the spirit of the law, they still had a responsibility to the family. When Boaz approaches the nearer kinsman he tells him first about the land without mentioning Ruth. The nearer kinsman assumes Naomi is the widow in question. Because she is past childbearing years, he also assumes she will not have an heir. Therefore, if he redeems the property, it will stay in his possession. That looks good to him. Is his motive noble (to care for the widow) or selfish (to get the land)? Boaz's approach reveals the motive of the man.

Read Ruth 4:1-4.

7.   What does Boaz say to the nearer kinsman? Note his diplomacy.

How does the nearer kinsman at first respond? (verse 4)

Read Ruth 4:5-8.

8.   What else does Boaz now tell the nearer kinsman? And how does the kinsman respond?

How does this reveal the motive of the nearer kinsman?

9.   The nearer kinsman removed his sandal (being barefoot was a stigma of unfaithfulness). How does Deuteronomy 25:5-10 show that though he was free to deny the widow, that still, it was a disgrace?

Read Ruth 4:9-10.

10. This transaction could have turned out differently than Boaz hoped, but Boaz still does what he believes is right before God. His faith is now rewarded. What does he now say and how does he show exuberance?

11. What principles do you see from the above in dealing with the world or with worldly believers?

Day 4: To the Faithful God Shows Himself Faithful

The Book of Ruth continually contrasts those who tried to save themselves with those who died to themselves.

12. According to the following passages, what is God's response to faith and selflessness? To fear and selfishness?
    A. 2 Samuel 22:26-28

    B. Matthew 6:33

    C. Matthew 10:39

13. How do you see fear or faith in the following people? Selflessness or selfishness? What is God's response to them?
    A. Elimelech and Boaz

    B. Orpah and Ruth

    C. Boaz and the nearer kinsman

Review your memory work.

14. Is there an area in your life where you could better exercise faith? Selflessness? Be specific.

Read Ruth 4:9-12.

15. The witnesses in Bethlehem, who admire Ruth and Boaz, break out into spontaneous praise and prayer. What do they say?

16. In their prayer they mention Judah, who, like the nearer kinsman, stands in an unfavorable light when compared to Boaz. Read the story in Genesis 38:6-30.

    A. What happened to Judah's first son and why? (verses 6-7)

    B. What happened to Judah's second son and why? (verses 8-10)

    C. Why do you think it was wicked of Onan to spill his seed?

Some have called this the sin of contraception. I see it as the sin of selfishness, rooted in a lack of faith. Onan did not honor the moral law of God, nor his father, nor his brother, nor his brother's widow because he didn't see anything in this arrangement for himself.

    D. What lie did Judah then tell Tamar? What motivated his lie? (verse 11)

    E. How did God show Himself shrewd to Judah? (verses 12-30)

    F. How does Boaz compare favorably to Judah?

Carrying on the name of the late kinsman was voluntary. Neither Judah nor the nearer kinsman had to do it. To do so was a sacrifice and an act of faith. It showed "hesed" and honored God. Boaz chose, because of love, to be a redeemer.

Day 5: The Wedding

Boaz and Ruth, because of their noble character, are especially loved and respected, so joy abounds at this wedding. There is also mighty prayer. The people know that Ruth was barren in Moab, and so they pray, and HOW THEY PRAY! They pray they will have many children (like Rachel and Leah) and that the children will be famous (have standing in Bethlehem).

This exemplifies a wedding that honors God. God's will has been sought and now witnesses actively participate in the wedding through prayer. In courageous faith they call upon God to show Himself faithful to the faithful.

David Atkinson says:

In our day, marriage is coming to be thought of by some only as a private alliance between two people, to be made (and even terminated) as they wish, by their private choice. But society has always had an interest in the formation of a new pair bond, and the growth of a new family unit in society.[52]

Marriage is God's holy ordinance, and a marriage (or a divorce) impacts many more people than just the bride and groom. Therefore a wedding *should involve the community* as it does here. The enormous opportunity of having believers pray for the couple should be seized (bridal showers are another opportunity). Then, in the future, the community of believers has a continued responsibility to support the marriage through prayer and encouragement.

17. What can you glean as the purpose for involving the community of believers in a wedding from Ruth 4:9-12?

Weddings are important to God. Jesus began His ministry at a wedding and will close with a wedding. For when He comes back, He is coming as a Bridegroom for His bride. Weddings should be both a festive and a serious time, as that great day will be.

18. (Challenge question!) How might an earthly wedding be a reflection of the day Jesus comes back for His bride?

To answer this question, in addition to the spirit of the wedding, you might consider the meaning behind a virginal bride, a white wedding gown, the trumpet before the processional, a wedding banquet, etc.

19. According to Ephesians 5:21-35, how can an earthly marriage be a reflection of the relationship between Jesus and true believers (the church)?

How do you see this in the relationship of Boaz and Ruth?

20. If you were helping to plan a shower or a wedding, what would be some festive and God-honoring ideas?

21. How might you pray for the bride and groom scripturally?

Day 6: Naomi Has a Son!

Ruth fills Naomi's empty arms with the ultimate gift. It is interesting because the witnesses say "Naomi has a son!" As the godly Boaz took both women into his home, Naomi is alone no more, her empty arms are full, she is embraced by a family, by the community of believers, and her future is hopeful. What a lovely family portrait showing the power of God to the faithful with which to close this book of *"hesed."*

Read Ruth 4:13-22.

22. How do you see the prayers of the believers at the wedding being answered in verse 13? In verse 22?

23. If you have friends struggling with infertility, how could you help them? (If there is someone in your group who has experienced this personally, encourage her to share what helps and what does not help.)

What would be a wise way to pray?

Occasionally when touching on this subject in my speaking, the Spirit prompts me to pray, from the podium, for those experiencing this very painful situation. Often I pray that God will either give them the desire of their heart or change the desire of their heart (Psalm 34:4). Recently a woman came up to me who had been present when I prayed that way five years earlier. She said: "I had had six miscarriages. When you prayed that way, suddenly an overwhelming peace came over me. I have not been able to conceive again, but I have had a peace. I am not imagining it, neither could I have drummed it up. That peace is a gift from God."

24. Describe the praise, prayer, and prophecy of the women at the house that day.

What stands out to you and why?

25. This story illustrates Psalm 68:6. Explain how.

If you have a husband and children, have you "adopted" any people who are single? If so, share something about it.

26. How do the women of Bethlehem give a gentle rebuke to Naomi? (verse 15)

What have you seen in particular in the life of Ruth which you admire? (Instead of just saying "love" or "faith," be passionate and specific. For example, "I'll never forget how she kept on loving Naomi even when Naomi hurt her feelings!")

27. How do you desire to follow Ruth's example in your own life?

Blessing Time

Have each woman, one by one, kneel in the center of a circle. (For time's sake, you may want to break into circles of four or five.) As she kneels, she should share her answer to question 27. All place their hands on her and pray silently. Two or three should pray aloud with sentence prayers. When there is silence she should rise and another woman should take her place.

Eight

I Will Sing of My Redeemer

At the close of the story, the women friends of Naomi surround her as she cradles Obed and say:

Praise be to the Lord, who this day has not left you without a kinsman-redeemer (Ruth 4:14).

We too should cry, "Thanks be to God, who has not left us without a Kinsman-Redeemer!" Like Ruth, we were aliens, "foreigners to the covenants of the promise, without hope and without God in the world" (Ephesians 2:12). But because God loved us so, He sent a Kinsman-Redeemer to earth, so that now in Christ Jesus we "who once were far away have been brought near through the blood of Christ" (Ephesians 2:13).

The Old Testament is like a picture book; the New Testament provides the captions. When I consider the interweaving of the historical story of Ruth with the symbolism of the land (the famine, the harvest) and the prophetic picture of Jesus as our Kinsman-Redeemer, I am overwhelmed. I think, "How did You do that, Lord?" When I reflect on the magnitude of God, I echo the thoughts of David in Psalm 8:3-4:

When I consider Your heavens,
the work of Your fingers,
the moon and the stars,
which You have set in place,
what is man that You are mindful of him?

Yet, the good news is that God *is* mindful of us. Jesus was willing to leave His throne in heaven. He was willing to take on the form of man, the form of a servant, to be our Kinsman. He paid dearly to redeem us, not with silver or gold, but with His precious blood (1 Peter 1:18-19). Praise be to God, who has not left us without a Kinsman-Redeemer!

Prepare Your Heart to Hear
Sing "Open My Eyes, Lord" from your hymnal, each day, before you study.

Memory Work
Review Ruth 1:16-17 and Ruth 2:10-12. (Review these for the next five years at Thanksgiving and they will be yours forever.)

Warm-Up
God places great value on the *family* of God. We are to value our relationship as sisters in Christ. In one breath, share one way the sisters in this small group have blessed you.

Day 1: Overview
The most obvious symbolism in the Book of Ruth is that of the kinsman-redeemer. Most theologians agree that Boaz is a Christ-figure. In addition to the kinsman-redeemer image, Boaz represented Christ in other ways. He gave Ruth rest, which Christ says He will do for any who come to Him. ("Come to Me, all you who are weary and burdened, and I will give you rest," Matthew 11:28.) Boaz told Ruth to help herself to the water jars whenever she was thirsty, and Christ promises that "whoever drinks the water I give him will never thirst" (John 4:14). Boaz invited Ruth to eat at his table, as Christ invites us to His table (1 Corinthians 10:21).

1. What stood out to you from the Introduction (pp. 98-99)?

Read through the Book of Ruth one last time for this study. Consider the helpless situation of Ruth, the lost inheritance of Naomi, the kindness of Boaz, and the rejoicing of the community. Consider the spiritual parallels.

2. What did you notice that you haven't noticed before?

Review your memory passages.

Day 2: Jesus Our Kinsman

While growing up, I was jealous of my two popular older sisters (the Homecoming Queens!) and I tried to make their lives miserable! Did they cut me out of their lives? NO! If I had been a friend, they might have, but I am their SISTER, so they gave me grace. Studies show that only 3 percent of sibling bonds permanently disconnect. Blood bonds are STRONG!

The Book of Ruth shows the strong sense of family solidarity among the people of Yahweh. They had a duty to care for each other. The law of the "kinsman-redeemer" reflected that.

Jesus became one of us, and if we have trusted in His blood sacrifice, He is "not ashamed to call us brothers" (Hebrews 2:11). J. Vernon McGee says this puts a heart into redemption.

> *A mother is willing to sacrifice herself for the child at her bosom because the little one is flesh of her flesh. . . . Blood relationship begets in the heart an affection and love that is sometimes beyond human comprehension.*[53]

Jesus almost invariably described Himself on earth as the "Son of Man." He is our brother, our Kinsman.

3. Think of a blood relative to whom you are close. Describe your bond.

With this in mind, what does it mean to you that Jesus became your Kinsman?

Read Ruth 2:13.

In the *King James Version,* the above verse says: "for that thou hast comforted me, and for that thou hast spoken friendly unto thine handmaid, though I be not like unto one of thine handmaidens." It overwhelms me, personally, when Jesus "speaks friendly to me." He is so holy and I am so sinful, yet He calls me, as Boaz did with Ruth, "My daughter" (Ruth 2:8; 3:10).

4. If possible, share a time when you sensed that Jesus "spoke friendly" to you or when you sensed He was treating you like "a daughter."

5. Read Hebrews 2 prayerfully and then answer:
    A. What passage from Psalms is repeated in verses 6-8?

    B. What do we learn about Jesus becoming our Kinsman in verses 9-12?

    C. What are some of the reasons that Jesus became our Kinsman according to verses 14-18?

Personal Action Assignment
Jesus understands your weaknesses, because He shared in your humanity. Pray through Hebrews 4:15-16 in thanksgiving. Then tell Jesus your weaknesses and ask Him for grace to change.

Day 3: Jesus, Our Redeemer
Ruth was helpless, outcast, under the curse. As a Moabitess, she was not allowed to enter the assembly of the Lord even unto the tenth generation. But the curse is broken. She enters in, becomes an ancestor of Christ, and has her name listed in the genealogy of Christ (Matthew 1:5). Why? Because Ruth is no longer a Moabitess. Ruth is redeemed, covered in righteousness. The book which began with famine and death ends with plenty and new life.

The baby born to Ruth and Boaz will become the grandfather of David. And out of David, and the city of David, will come forth one whose origins have been from of old, from everlasting.

6.   Describe the helplessness of Ruth as a Moabite widow.

Describe our helplessness before a Holy God and our bondage in sin (Romans 3:23; John 8:34).

7.   Explain how the transaction that Boaz made to redeem Ruth was a public transaction (Ruth 4).

Explain how the transaction that Jesus made to redeem us was a public transaction. (See John 3:14 and John 12:32-33.)

8.   Explain how the transaction that Boaz made to redeem Ruth was costly (Ruth 3:9).

Explain how the transaction that Jesus made to redeem us was much more costly. (See 1 Peter 1:18-19.)

9.   What did Naomi gain because Boaz paid the price of redemption?

What can we gain because Jesus paid the price for our redemption? (See Colossians 1:12-14.)

What can we gain because Jesus paid the price for our redemption? (See Colossians 1:12-14.)

Some godly men, such as M.R. De Haan (The Romance of Redemption) *have seen a prophetic parable in Ruth. We need to be very careful in drawing allegories from Scripture when the text itself does not claim to be an allegory, for we may be led astray in doing so. We need to emphasize instead God's clear and intended teaching. However, though God may not have intended Ruth to be a parable, I agree with those who say it has helped them to understand the past and future of God's people. The Israelites were scattered because of disobedience (as Naomi's family was), Gentiles were then grafted into the family (as Ruth was), and eventually there will be restoration for the Jews (as Naomi was restored to the family).*

Day 4: Review: Hesed in Naomi

The Book of Ruth has been called the book of *hesed*, of "unfailing love." There are two concepts intertwined in this great Hebrew word: *kindness* (or mercy) and *steadfastness*. *Hesed* is what every single person desires from God and from their loved ones (Proverbs 19:22a). We want our loved ones to be kind and merciful to us and to never give up on us. God always gives *hesed* and He longs for us to give it to one another, but it is actually very rare (Proverbs 20:6). In the days of the Judges there were very few who showed *hesed*. But God has always had a remnant, and shining in those dark days were Naomi, Ruth, and Boaz. To be sure you have understood and embraced the central message of the book, do these last three days thoughtfully.

Naomi is the central character in the Book of Ruth. Everything and everyone revolves around her. Elimelech is defined as "Naomi's husband," Orpah and Ruth as "Naomi's daughters-in-law," and Boaz as "Naomi's relative." *Hesed* begins with Naomi in the opening of the book as she gives this unfailing love to her Moabite daughters-in-law. And *hesed* comes back full circle to Naomi at the close of the book in the idyllic scene with her friends, family, and newborn grandson.

Meditate on God's hesed (unfailing love) by singing "Great Is Thy Faithfulness" from your hymnal.

10. *Hesed* is used to describe the love of the Lord. How do you see both kindness and steadfastness in Lamentations 3:22-23?

Which aspect of *hesed* do you see most clearly personified in Naomi (kindness or steadfastness)? Explain.

11. Kindness is voluntary. Naomi did not have to accept her Moabite daughters-in-law, but she did. Why was this remarkable? (Review Day 5 from Lesson 1.)

12. Review the evidence from Ruth 1 that Naomi loved and blessed her daughters-in-law.

There is great power in the kind of love demonstrated in the Book of Ruth. Likewise, there can be great harm wrought through the lack of "hesed." (Philip Yancey calls this "ungrace" in What's So Amazing About Grace?*) When we give "ungrace" we bring great pain to ourselves, our relationships, and to future generations. It's painful to forgive when we have been wronged. "The only thing harder than forgiveness is the alternative."[54]*

13. How was Naomi blessed by giving grace? How did it eventually lead to her restoration?

What might have happened to Naomi had she refused to embrace Ruth and Orpah? What do you learn from this?

14. Are there people in your life to whom you have difficulty giving grace? Specifically how could you give them grace?

15. What will you remember about Naomi's model of *hesed*?

Day 5: Review: Hesed in Ruth

The example of Ruth comes to my mind nearly every day of my life. I am so thankful for her example of steadfast love and its power in breaking down walls. When I am rejected, whether it is by a daughter who is dealing with the pain of spending her childhood in an orphanage or by a friend who is dealing with a storm within, I remember Ruth. Five times Naomi rejected her. Never does Ruth lash out. Never does Ruth retreat. She just keeps on loving, and in due time, she sees a harvest.

The hardest time to give unfailing love is when we feel unappreciated, yet, if we do not give up, we will bear fruit.

Prepare your heart by singing "Love Divine, All Loves Excelling" and "Beloved, Let Us Love One Another" from your hymnal.

16. Describe the warning and the promise given in Galatians 6:7-10.

How is Ruth an example of the above promise?

17. Review Ruth 1 and find the five rejections from Naomi.

    Describe Ruth's response. Why do you think Ruth was able to respond as she did?

Not even Abraham's leap of faith surpasses this decision of Ruth's. And there is more. Not only has Ruth broken with family, country and faith, but she has also reversed sexual allegiance. A young woman has committed herself to the life of an old woman rather than to the search for a husband. . . . One female has chosen another female in a world where life depends upon men. There is no more radical decision in all the memories of Israel.[55]

18. How do you respond when someone rejects you?

    What could you learn from Ruth?

19. List all the ways in which Ruth filled up Naomi's empty arms. Give verse references.

20. List all the ways God blessed Ruth for her unfailing love. Give verse references.

21. What do you think you will remember from the example of Ruth?

Day 6: Review: Hesed in Boaz

The magnanimity of Boaz knows no bounds. He does not have to do what he freely chooses to do, which is to provide for Ruth, protect her, marry her, and embrace not only her, but her mother-in-law. A key aspect of *hesed* is that it is voluntary, which is what makes it so amazing.

Glimmering beneath the figure of Boaz is our wonderful Lord. He did not have to leave His throne in heaven, but He chose to come to earth and become our Kinsman. Likewise, He did not have to die for us, but He chose to be our Redeemer.

Prepare your heart by singing "I Will Sing of My Redeemer." (Text at close of this lesson.)

22. How did you see unfailing love in Boaz? Give verse references.

23. How did God bless Boaz because of his unfailing love?

24. What do you think you will remember from the example of Boaz?

25. How do you see Jesus glimmering beneath the figure of Boaz?

26. Describe the song that is sung about our Kinsman-Redemmer in Revelation 5:9-10.

27. Write down several ways your life is different because you have a Kinsman-Redeemer. (From what has He freed you? What have you inherited?)

Prayer Time

In circles of four or five, have one woman read the passage. Then allow women to pray about the passage in regard to themselves—either in praise, confession, or supplication.

1. Lamentations 3:22-23
Because of the Lord's great love we are not consumed, for His compassions never fail. They are new every morning; great is Your faithfulness.

2. 1 John 4:7-8
Dear friends, let us love one another, for love comes from God. Everyone who loves has been born of God and knows God. Whoever does not love does not know God, because God is love.

3. Galatians 6:9
Let us not become weary in doing good, for at the proper time we will reap a harvest if we do not give up.

4. 1 Peter 1:17-19
Since you call on a Father who judges each man's work impartially, live your lives as strangers here in reverent fear. For you know that it was not with perishable things such as silver or gold that you were redeemed from the empty way of life handed down to you from your forefathers, but with the precious blood of Christ, a lamb without blemish or defect.

5. Ruth 4:14a
Praise be to the Lord, who this day has not left you without a Kinsman-Redeemer.

Close with the first verse and chorus from "I Will Sing of My Redeemer"

I Will Sing of My Redeemer

I will sing of my Redeemer and His wondrous love to me;
On the cruel cross He suffered, from the curse to set me free.

Chorus:
Sing, O sing of my Redeemer,
With His blood He purchased me;
On the cross He sealed my pardon,
Paid the debt and made me free.

I will tell the wondrous story, how, my lost estate to save,
In His boundless love and mercy, He the ransom freely gave.

I will praise my dear Redeemer, His triumphant power I'll tell,
How the victory He giveth over sin and death and hell.

I will sing of my Redeemer and His heavenly love to me;
He from death to life hath brought me, Son of God with Him to be.

Sources

Introduction
1.   Jan Titterington, "Insights from the Book of Ruth," *His.* January 1976, 3.

One: In the Days When the Judges Ruled
2.   John W. Reed, *The Bible Knowledge Commentary. Old Testament.* Eds. John F. Walvoord and Roy B. Zuck (Wheaton, Ill.: Victor Books, 1985), 415.
3.   Lawrence O. Richards, *The Bible Reader's Companion* (Wheaton, Ill.: Victor Books, 1991), 157.
4.   Kenneth R.R. Gros Louis, "The Book of Judges." *Literary Interpretations of Biblical Narratives.* Ed. Kenneth R.R. Gros Louis (Nashville: Abingdon Press, 1974), 147.
5.   Dr. A.C. Hervey, "Judges." *The Pulpit Commentary.* Vol. 3. Ed. H.D.M. Spence and Joseph S. Excell (Peabody, Mass.: Hendrickson, n.d.), 194–95.
6.   "Moab." *The International Standard Bible Encyclopedia.* Vol. 3. Eds. Geoffrey W. Bromiley, Roland K. Harrison, and Williiam Sanford Lasor (Grand Rapids: William B. Eerdmans Publishing, 1986), 393.
7.   "Moabite Stone." *Unger's Bible Dictionary* (Chicago: Moody, 1966), 755–56.
8.   "Moab." *The International Standard Bible Encyclopedia*, 395.
9.   "Moabite." *Unger's Bible Dictionary*, 754
10. "Moab." *The International Standard Bible Encyclopedia*, 395.

Two: Love in a Time of Famine
11. Joyce G. Baldwin, "Ruth." *New Bible Commentary.* 4th ed. Eds. D.A. Carson, R.T. France, J.A. Motyer, and G.J. Wenham (Downers Grove, Ill.: InterVarsity, 1994), 287.
12. D.F. Rauber, "The Book of Ruth." *Literary Interpretations of Biblical Narratives*, 165–67.
13. M.R. DeHaan, *The Romance of Redemption: Studies in the Book of Ruth*, 37.
14. Helmut Thielicke, *The Waiting Father.* trans. by John W. Doberstein (New York: Harper, 1959), 24–26.
15. Matthew Henry, "Joshua to Esther." *Matthew Henry's Commentary on the Whole Bible.* Vol. 2 (Peabody, Mass.: Hendrickson, 1991), 198.
16. Cyril J. Barber, *Ruth: An Expositional Commentary* (Chicago: Moody, 1983), 44.

17. Gwen Shamblin, *The Weigh Down Diet* (New York: Doubleday, 1997), 151.
18. Ruth Anna Putnam, "Friendship." *Reading Ruth: Contemporary Women Reclaim a Sacred Story.* Ed. Judith A. Kates and Gail Twersky Reimer (New York: Ballantine Books, 1994), 45.
19. Gary Smalley and John Trent, Ph.D., *Leaving the Light On* (Sisters, Ore.: Multnomah, 1994), 162.
20. Craig S. Keener, *...And Marries Another: Divorce and Remarriage in the Teaching of the New Testament* (Peabody, Mass.: Hendrickson, 1991), 82.
21. R.C. Sproul. *Now That's a Good Question!* (Wheaton, Ill.: Tyndale House, 1996), 380–81.
22. Gary Smalley and John Trent, Ph.D., *The Blessing* (New York: Pocket Books, 1986), 136–37.
23. Samuel Cox, as quoted in Cyril J. Barber, *Ruth: An Expositional Commentary*, 55.

Three: But Ruth Clung to Her

24. Murray D. Gowan, *The Book of Ruth: Its Structure, Theme and Purpose* (Leicester, England: Apollos), 1992, 34.
25. Henry Moorhouse, *Ruth, The Moabitess: Gleanings from the Book of Ruth* (Chicago: The Bible Institute Colportage Association, 1881), 11.
26. J. Vernon McGee, *Ruth: The Romance of Redemption*, 62.
27. Morning Star Prophetic Tape of the Month, March 1998.
28. Walter Trobisch, *I Married You* (New York: HarperSanFrancisco, 1971), 19.
29. Ibid., 20.
30. J. Vernon McGee, *Ruth: The Romance of Redemption*, 61.
31. Avivah Zornberg, "The Concealed Alternative." *Reading Ruth: Contemporary Women Reclaim a Sacred Story*, 66.
32. Jan Titterington, "Insights from the Book of Ruth," *His*, 4.
33. Alicia Ostriker, "The Redeeming of Ruth." *Reading Ruth: Contemporary Women Reclaim a Sacred Story*, 89.
34. Nehama Aschkenasy, "Language as Female Empowerment in Ruth." *Reading Ruth: Contemporary Women Reclaim a Sacred Story*, 113.

Four: Giving Your Mother-in-Law Grace

35. Philip Yancey, *What's So Amazing about Grace?* (Grand Rapids: Zondervan, 1997), 100.
36. David Atkinson, *The Message of Ruth: The Wings of Refuge* (Downers Grove, Ill.: InterVarsity, 1983), 46–47.

37. Gloria Golreich, "Ruth, Naomi, and Orpah: A Parable of Friendship." *Reading Ruth: Contemporary Women Reclaim a Sacred Story*, 38.

38. Ruth H. Sohn, "Verse by Verse: A Modern Commentary." *Reading Ruth: Contemporary Women Reclaim a Sacred Story*, 20.

39. Dr. Lois C. Dubin, "Fullness and Emptiness, Fertility and Loss: Meditations on Naomi's Tale in the Book of Ruth." *Reading Ruth: Contemporary Women Reclaim a Sacred Story*, 135.

40. Dr. Joel D. Block and Diane Greenberg, as quoted in Dee Brestin, *The Friendships of Women* (Colorado Springs: Chariot Victor, 1997), 130.

41. Walter Trobisch, *I Married You*, 17.

42. Merle Field, "At the Crossroads." *Reading Ruth: Contemporary Women Reclaim a Sacred Story*, 174.

Five: Under His Wings

43. G. Campbell Morgan, as quoted in Cyril J. Barber, *Ruth: An Expositional Commentary*, 33.

44. Samuel Cox, as quoted in Cyril J. Barber, *Ruth: An Expositional Commentary*, 71.

45. Robert Watson, as quoted in J. Vernon McGee, *Ruth: The Romance of Redemption*, 76.

46. J. Vernon McGee, *Ruth: The Romance of Redemption*, 78.

47. David Atkinson, *The Message of Ruth: The Wings of Refuge*, 64.

48. Cyril J. Barber, *Ruth: An Expositional Commentary*, 88.

49. Bob Schwartz, *Diets Don't Work* (Houston: Breakthru, 1982), 80.

Six: My Daughter, Should I Not Try to Find a Home for You?

50. J. Vernon McGee, *Ruth: The Romance of Redemption*, 88, 93.

51. Cyril J. Barber, *Ruth: An Expositional Commentary*, 101.

Seven: Your Daughter-in-Law Is Better to You Than Seven Sons

52. David Atkinson, *The Message of Ruth: The Wings of Refuge*, 116.

Eight: Jesus, Our Kinsman Redeemer

53. J. Vernon McGee, *Ruth: The Romance of Redemption*, 138.

54. Philip Yancey, *What's So Amazing About Grace?* 45.

55. P. Trible, as quoted in Frederic W. Bush, "Esther." *Word Biblical Commentary*, Vol. 9. Ed. David A. Hubbard, Glen W. Barker, and John D.W. Watts (Dallas: Word, 1996), 54.

Combat Survival

Life Stories from a Purple Heart

Vietnam to Kenya to the Hood

George P. Hutchings
Former U.S. Marine Sergeant

D0668405

Combat Survival

Life Stories from a Purple Heart

Vietnam to Kenya to the Hood

George P. Hutchings
Former U.S. Marine Sergeant

Combat Survival - Life Stories from a Purple Heart
Vietnam to Kenya to the Hood
by George P. Hutchings
400 Tumulty, Ballwin, MO 63021
636-394-0310

Library of Congress

BIOGRAPHY/INSPIRATIONAL/ HISTORY

ISBN 0-9753455-9-1

Photo Credits:
Jim Morris, The Devils Secret Game (St. Martin's Paperback, 175 Fifth Avenue, New York, NY 10010): Corbis-page 1, 68; John Devaney, The Vietnam War (Franklin Watts, NY): Veterans of Foreign Wars; Map by William J. Clipson-page 34,backcover; AP/Wide World Photos-page 14, 30, 58, 70, 82, 84, backcover; James H. Pickerell-page 12, 52, 66, 76, backcover; Woodfin Camp & Associates-page 48; The John F. Kennedy Library; UPI/Bettmann Newsphotos-page 42, 50, 78, backcover; Edward C. Britton, Sacramento, CA-page 10, 44, 54, 62, backcover; Tom Myers, Sacramento, CA-page 86; Archive Photos, NY-page 40, 80, backcover; Gamma-Liaison/Francolor-page 64; ProFiles West/Frank Staub-page 88; George P. Hutchings-page 18, 20, 22, 24, 26, 28, 30, 32, 60, 72, 74.

Amerisearch, Inc.
P.O. Box 20163, St. Louis, MO 63123
1-888-USA-WORD, 314-487-4395 voice/fax

To my friends Craig & Jennifer,
God Bless
George Weathering
3/28/07

To all the men and women
who dared taste
the heat of battle
and smell the stench of blood.
Thank you.

CONTENTS

PREFACE

I hope this book will make you laugh and cry. Some of the names have been changed because it serves no purpose to hold teenage actions against 60 year old men. The boys of my teenage years are now hopefully my friends; I would do nothing to hinder those relationships. The fact is: kids are sometimes very cruel, but hopefully they mature and like a fine wine becoming tasteful. And during my life I have often committed terrible sins; I seek redemption and must therefore offer redemption.

PROLOGUE

In the military as in civilian life soldiers come in types:

1. The first man will dig into the fox hole with you, but when the enemy comes he runs.

2. The second man will dig into the fox hole but complains so much you wish he would run.

3. The third man digs in and stays for the fight. In thirty-five years of ministry I have found that Marines know the meaning of Semper Fi but very few Christian Soldiers can conceive the concept.

Sometimes a military motto is based on Christian teaching: "Semper Fi," Latin for 'Always Faithful.' This Marine Corps Doctrine could have been scripture based. "Never allow your friends to bleed to death on the battle field." Private Roy Munson and Captain Jack Ruffer did this for me on the battlefields of Vietnam and Richard Kim has done this for me on the battlefield of faith. Battlefields give rise to heroes and cowards. The men mentioned above are my hero's.

A more civilian interpretation of "Semper Fi," might be: Above all, a woman wants one thing from her man, faithfulness. If a man does not have faithfulness nothing else matters. "A man is defined not by what he thinks, but what he does," Batman.

Faithfulness is the fiber that holds life together.

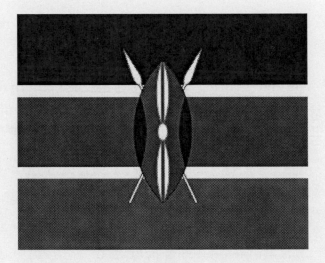

CHAPTER 1
ANY PLACE BUT AFRICA

March 1972, my faith had just been activated and the first thing I said was, "Lord I'll go anywhere you send me except Africa." Why did I make this a condition of following the Lord? Because there was an intuitive knowledge that someday I would be there and I didn't want to travel to the land of cannibals and warring tribes.

In May of the same year Dr. Sutherland, President of Missouri Baptist University (MBU) and my English teacher spoke to the class about the power of international personal relationships. Dr. Sutherland listed ten rouge nations. He pointed out that in all ten cases the leaders of those nations had been educated in the United States. The point was this: If Christian people had embraced these leaders with friendship such as: Invitations to eat in their own homes- would they still be the leaders of rouge nations? It is hard to declare war on friends.

I knew that someday, international students would be included in my ministry.

Early November, 1997 John Kihumba of Kenya attended a birthday party for a man named Doug. Doug made a point of his being an atheistic but gave John his number incase he ever needed help. John had been in the United States for over 30 days and had not reported to MBU. He was told by his friend Jessica that a black man walking down the streets of St. Louis would be arrested.

Jessica (a friend from Kenya) had had John wire his tuition money to her and now was trying to have him deported by not allowing him to report to school. John had sixty days to report to school or he would be deported. At this birthday party he realized the evil plot and confronted Jessica. It was a snowy December midnight and she kicked him out of the house suit case and all.

John had only one number, and two quarters. He called Doug and was picked up within thirty minutes. Doug's cousin Gloria overheard the conversation. She had followed my international ministry and called asking if she could give John my number. I said, "Yes."

December 18, 1997 at 8:28 PM, Mr. John Kihumba came to my office for financial assistance to continue his education at MBU. The conversation went something like this: "I am out of work, out of school, almost out of status."

"The tuition that I had saved for seven years was wired to Jessica, my friend from Kenya. She was to make the tuition payment. However, Jessica kept the money and told me that a Black man walking on the streets of St. Louis would be arrested."

"Jessica had a plan to keep me out of school for 60 days. I would then be deported and she could keep the money."

I was thinking, "Is this a fantastic story?" I asked John if he had reported to school. He said, "Yes." He showed me a class schedule. I asked John to get a letter of recommendation from one of the professors. He did so and returned within a couple of days. I sat silent; no one spoke for about three minutes. Then I uttered the words, "John you have so many problems." John was thinking I know I have problems; I came all this way to have this man tell me I have problems. He must be the wrong man.

Then it came to me, "But John you have a God who is bigger than all your problems." He hugged me and we began working. The school traced the funds and found his story to be true. We went on the speaking circuit and raised immediate money for rent and food. Within a month, John was working and back on his feet.

One of the ways John supported himself was trash cans. People would throw out old or broken computers. John was a computer science major and when he saw the power cord of a computer coming from a trash can he ask the resident if he could have the discarded computer. Many times the homeowner would tell John that if he could fix it, they would pay him. Later, I would find that this is typical of Kenya people.

They overcome problems.

Spring 1998, John came to me in a panic. The American Embassy in Nairobi had been bombed and John had a two year old boy, Alexam, still in Kenya. Immediately we sponsored a golf tournament and raised enough money for Peter, John's brother, to fly himself and Alexam to America.

The plane was in Chicago when we found out that Peter was arriving in St. Louis without the child. John and Damaris (John's wife) hearts hung low. Peter was now approaching us from the plane without Alexam. I told him get back on the plane and don't come back without the child. I knew that was impossible but wanted to let Peter know his incompetence had wasted our funds. What had gone wrong?

John was to have paid a dowry for Damaris but had not finished the payments to the parents. A former Kenya tradition had carried over to John's situation. In Kenya a dowry is paid for a daughter because a daughter works providing income for the family. The parents left without a daughter have loss income. A dowry paid especially in cattle and goats provide a continual income.

At the last minute the grandparents decided to keep the boy until the final dowry payment was made. The grandparents did not bring Alexam to the airport and Peter failed to change his date of departure. Two tickets or about $4000 was wasted.

Then I turned to John and Damaris and said, "We don't have time to be depressed, let's kick the devil in the ass and go get that boy. How? I had no idea. But leaving a child on the battlefield was not my style.

We returned to the church speaking circuit and raised enough money to fly John to Kenya and return with the child himself.

Another problem in Kenya was that there were no American Embassy services to grant visas to American. John and Alexam flew to France. The Kenya authorities told him that he would not have a visa to travel from France to America. John said, "Just get me that visa and I'll figure it out as we go." He was granted the visa to France.

France would not give the pair a visa to America. One security guard gave John a note to return to the diplomatic window. He was to go there to be deported back to Kenya. However, the attendant only noticed, "DIPLOMATE."

He thought John was a diplomat and stamped his visa to the United States. A group of people came out to help with the luggage and the son. Within one hour John and Alexam were on a plane to America.

The pair landed on American soil on the last day of John's 120 or he would have never been allowed back in the country.

That crisis was over. Whew! And I had still not traveled to Africa. And I had not even thought about such travel.

The phone rang and it was Bob Kupp a former career missionary to Kenya. He asked if I want to make a mission trip to Kenya with him.

Immediately, I said no. I don't know anyone in Kenya and I only work along lines of personal relationships. We hung up.

I looked across the table and there was John Kihumba from Kenya. "John, do you know any reason why we should make a mission trip to Kenya? He picked up my phone and called international long distant to Margaret Magugue. He had once fixed her computer and charged her nothing. This type of Christian action is unheard of in Kenya. Of course, Margaret remembered him. Margaret was married to Author Magugue the former financial secretary of Kenya and good friend of President Moi.

Author instructed me to write a letter to President Moi and indicated that he would deliver the letter.

Our public relations campaign had not even whispered but a man from Ballwin Baptist Church sold medical implements to doctors and began raising equipment for us. Lourdes Hospital in Paducah, Kentucky donated skids of equipment. The news spread and suddenly we had over $100,000 worth of medical supplies.

My letter to President Moi went this way: "Citizens of Kenya are inviting me to enter your country for the purpose of a Christian sponsored medical missionary trip. However, it is our policy to never cross international borders without the express permission of the highest government officials and work with them in accordance with their laws and under their watch care."

I received a letter from President Moi giving me permission. In 1999, we traveled to Kenya with $100,000 worth of medical supplies and presented it to the President. That night we appeared with him on national television and have been delivering medical supplies to him each year. We now have a standing agreement that as I find the medical supplies he pays the freight.

Much to my surprise Kenya was not filled with warring tribes and cannibals. One family wanted us to come over for dinner and I asked, "How many are going to eat us?"

The Kenya people were found to be the most gracious people on earth. If they don't have a bed, they thank God for a blanket. If they don't have a blanket they thank God for a spot on the floor. In Kenya people walk everywhere. I understand why: Our driver was excellent! There was only one pot hole in the road and he hit it 10,000 times.

The Kenya people find a way to make a living. In America we call this an entrepreneur. Kenya people are creative, industrious, and bear hardships with good humor. I love them.

My prayer has now become, "Lord, don't send me anywhere but Kenya."

Kenya is country of jungles that remind me of Vietnam. Kenya also is a country of pot holes and hospitable people. My previous experiences in Vietnam prepared me for jungles, fox holes, and hostility. The Kenya jungle and Swahili brought flashbacks of Vietnam memories. The Kenya hospitality far out weighted the hostility of Vietnam, but the flashbacks continued.

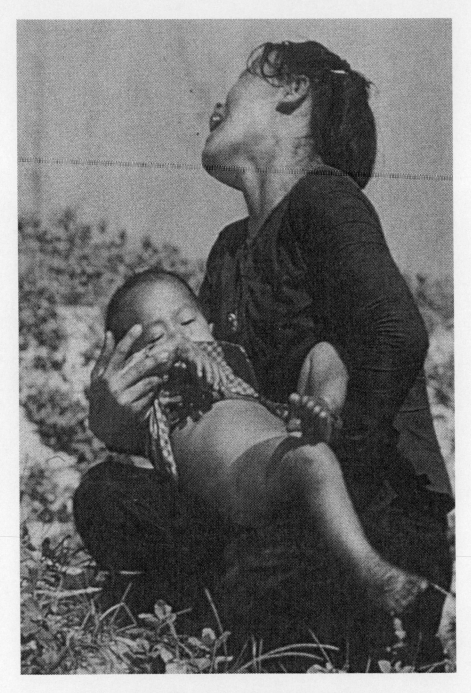

War always spills over on the civilian population.

GEORGE P. HUTCHINGS - COMBAT SURVIVAL

CHAPTER 2
BLOODY HANDS

June, 1967—Quang Tri Province, South Vietnam. I had the stripes but not the scars. Scars come only through experience. Scars earn respect. So, a more experienced Private First Class (PFC) was our squad leader, in spite of my rank. Though admittedly insecure with leadership, my ego and two stripes demanded respect.

Seeing a gook moving down a dirt path, I told my squad leader, "Shoot him!" The private declined my order, so I sighted down the barrel of my M-16. "If you won't ..." I said...

My weapon had not yet been fired and my time in country was about one month. A Marine returning home without the heat of battle would be laughed to scorn. Now the moment of opportunity had finally come. A 17 year-old kid from small-town USA was anxious to draw enemy blood and become a hero. Savoring the anticipated shot, the rifle had a chilling calmness to it as the stock pressed against my cheek.

Looking through the peep sight, my mind's eye didn't see a gook. I saw Oscar. He was my best buddy the summer before first grade. But when we started to school he spurned and scorned me, and spent the next twelve years gutting my social life. He should have been my best friend, but he became my worst enemy. Day after day, year after year, he had stolen away those who should have been my friends, stolen away all that should have been my life. One mocking blow after another, he had kicked a psychological blow through the heart of my life. A heart trained to hate prepared me for this day-the day of vengeance.

Battalion Supply Route

GEORGE P. HUTCHINGS - COMBAT SURVIVAL

My mind recalled the day I took my 12-guage shotgun to gym class to shoot Oscar and the rest of his basketball starter friends. That lust for revenge had held me in its vise all these years. I wanted revenge. But my family name and Catholic upbringing held the fiber of life together and I could not shoot. Suddenly, halfway around the world, a murder could now be committed in the name of righteous war, and my pain could be satisfied.

My target was about 500 yards away, behind a hedge. All I could see was the head and shoulders. The sight was on his head. I began to have second thoughts: "Should I shoot, or not? What's wrong?" Just as I had not fired on Oscar, I did not want to fire on an innocent civilian. The shooting had to be righteous. In boot came we learned on an M-14 to take up the trigger slack and ease the round. My M-16 did not have slack. While still wrestling with the dialogue in my head, the trigger released, and I felt a shock of surprise. An explosion rang and echoed down the canyon of my life. It wasn't the sound of a gunshot at a firing range. It was the sound of an explosion bursting through my hardened heart. The M-16 jammed and I fought to eject the round and insert another in the chamber.

The subject fell, and joy leaped within my heart. Victory! I recalled the emotions of squirrel hunting and ran to pick up my prey. But when we reached the site we found a pet water buffalo hidden behind the hedge. A young boy had been riding the buffalo, making him the height of a man. The men around me didn't see an armed Viet Cong, as I expected. Lying on the ground was a small innocent boy. This had been my prey. Pontius Pilate said, "I am innocent of His blood." The squad that surrounded Pontius Pilate knew otherwise. And I knew otherwise.

I did not volunteer for Vietnam to kill women and children and the Marine Corps never taught such actions. In war death spills over onto an innocent population.

The dead boy's mother ran from her bamboo hut. Her arms we extended and tears streamed over the shock of her face. Her sobbing was unlike anything I had ever heard. Somebody was screaming, though not in words, "You are supposed to be the good guys. What have you done?"

There had been two comforts in this mother's life a moment ago-the young boy and the bamboo hut to share with him. Now nothing of comfort was left. In her sobbing, I saw my own mother and brother, and my emotions staggered out of bounds. A young boy lay at my feet with the back of his head blown off.

This family hadn't asked for war; they probably didn't even understand it. This boy had done nothing to sentence him to a firing squad. But nothing could bring back the previous five minutes. Time went on as if the boy had never lived.

GEORGE P. HUTCHINGS - COMBAT SURVIVAL

All my life must pay
Just for one riotous day.
Years of regret and grief,
Sorrow without relief.
Suffer it I will, my friend,
Suffer it until the end,
Until the end will bring relief.
Dr. R.G. Lee

Corporal George P. Hutchings, serial number 2286590, had committed a mortal sin. I "Hung in the balance and was found wanting." Blood streamed from my hands and nothing could wash it away. My future was dark and my ears filled with the sound of a small voice, "Because of you, I am dead today."

And there was another voice of mocking irony: "The blood of this small, innocent boy hasn't even avenged your hatred." Psychologists would call this an act of sublimation: To be angry at one person and explode on another person. This act by any name was not heroic. I hung my head not excepting the surrounding confusion for excuses.

In the wake of that tragedy, I had to face Captain Bill Major, but someday, in my own death, I knew I would face a far more deadly judge. Hell waited.

Captain Bill Major conferred with the rest of the squad and knew it was an act of war. Marines are not trained to kill children, and I knew in my heart that I had shot at the enemy. But my conscience called it Bloody Hands, and more than one childhood had been murdered.

Experience had delivered its first savage scar.

George at the breakfast table before the war.

George's biggest concern was winning at baskeball. Soon he
would trade his number 53 jersey for serial number 2286590.

In war, three things cannot be captured in the motion pictures: the noise of battle, the impact of death falling like a guillotine, and the smell of blood.

In reality, the noise of battle displaces all private thought. And the startle of death delivers shock. Until I saw that small boy, I never knew shock.

A mother's soul cries out, "My son is gone. Who will take care of me in my old age?" Death had swept away her son. It would sweep her away. It would sweep me away. . In the blink of an eye, a person not only dies, but is also forgotten. "And there arose a Pharaoh who knew not Joseph."

Marine Boot Camp 1966

CHAPTER 3
STAND ON THE YELLOW FEET

From first grade until high school graduation, I was socially castrated one day at a time. Dr. Allen says the early years of life are the years that give rise to a neurotic personality. He also states that one cannot blame current failure on childhood scars. It seems we have the responsibility to "come to ourselves", push off the past and get on with living. Furthermore, we must accept the truth that parenting is always an experiment being performed by mortal people of widely varying ability, on kids of widely varying temperaments. Sometimes parents hit glorious home runs; sometimes they strike out in the most ridiculously foolish manner.

I was handy with a screwdriver and one day Mom's washing machine came apart. She was mad and blamed it on me. She interrogated me until the proper confession was made. Then she whipped the daylights out of me. A couple weeks later the same thing happened, but I wasn't around. She knew she had made a mistake the first time, and asked for forgiveness. What does a four-year-old know about bestowing forgiveness? Sure I forgave her; she stood over me like a giant. I would have done anything she wanted, but it was too late now to ever recover that quivering tenderness of worship.

I don't remember the details of that washing machine incident, but my emotions do. From time to time Mom still brings up this unpleasant experience and my mind forgives her. However, even after forgiveness is granted, emotions still evoke a reaction.

George at age ten makes a battle plan with brother Charlie.

Words, people, and circumstances detonate emotional scars. Sometimes just one word triggers an explosive memory. And emotions of rejection control without permission. This particular experience caused two emotional responses: for years, the word "Mom" brought fear, and I'm still afraid of tools.

To my Mom's great credit, she never let strike outs get the best of her. She built bridges over rips of hurt by baking the best bread, sweet rolls, and cakes. One of my fondest memories is licking cake icing from the bowl. When she really wanted to show how much she loved us, she made doughnuts. Picking tomatoes alongside her and eating them right from the garden was another warm bridge. But the sweetest times were the hours we spent together after I returned home from squirrel hunting. We would visit while she made breakfast.

The aroma of bacon, eggs, and freshly brewed coffee still reminds me that Mom hit many more home runs than strike outs. If she gave early scars, she also taught me to "Take another turn at the plate."

GEORGE P. HUTCHINGS - COMBAT SURVIVAL

And, admittedly, Mom often had provocation for her strikeout temper. When she wanted us to come in and do the dishes, we wanted to play until dark. It wasn't that we didn't want to do the dishes; we just wanted to do them after dark. But Mom always wanted them done right away. She was positive there was more to life than a whiffle ball game.

Mom and my brother, Charles, tell me I was the "Apple of Dad's eye." But my memories of him are quite different. I didn't feel like the apple of his eye so much as the scrutiny of his eye. When he was the principal of my school, he stood by the front door of the school with a club to punish those who ran. I came flying out the front door, he would send me back inside—so I ran out the back door. He was big, he had a club, and he was the boss. That's how I remember Dad. No memories of Dad are more vivid than the hours he spent trying to improve my reading.

I became his project. Being a man of poor health, Dad was impatient, and this increased my fear. Sick with worry because I didn't know the words, fear further froze my ability to learn. It was a sad cycle. Dad, in my eyes, was the smartest man in the world, and here I was, a disgrace, because I couldn't read. I was afraid he would think I was dumb. From then on, I was afraid of my father. He would never have hurt me, but I was desperately afraid of disappointing him. I wanted to measure up.

Dad tried to build bridges over the fears and difficult times, too, but my fear and his health blocked a bonding relationship. I don't remember a time when he didn't have heart and kidney problems. After one kidney operation, we were told not to hug him. Mom feared we would break the stitches. What translated to my emotions, however, was, "Keep away from Dad."

At age two George wore his father's Army drill instructor hat.

Dad's tender mercies came in the summer time. We lived in an old farmhouse that included a screened front porch with a swing. The days were hot, but the evenings were cool. Mom and Dad would sit in the porch swing while we lay on quilt pallets, and Dad, always the teacher, would read us a story. But sometimes he would tell us his own stories, and he would invent big whoppers. Dad's whoppers were better than television, probably because we did not own a television. He was our father and we hung on every word.

His favorite story was told in the presence of Grandma. He began by telling us he pitched baseball in high school. The school wasn't big enough to have nine players, so he had to pitch and catch. "I would throw a 90 mph fast ball, beat it to home plate, and throw it back to myself on the mound."

Dad continued, "Once, someone hit a ball to center field and I ran back to catch it. And then the third base runner headed. I threw to home place, beat the throw, picked up the catcher's mitt and tagged the runner out." Grandma said, "Really Paul!" He would smile, and everyone but Grandma knew they had been had.

Several years later, when returning home from boot camp, Dad wanted to test my mettle. He'd had his annual heart attack and was missing a kidney, but he put three left jabs on my chin before I could blink. He wanted to make sure I remembered he still pulled the punches. I remembered. I wish I could have mustered even a bit of my dad's sense of command and authority. Maybe then Oscar would have just been an annoying fly on the screened porch of my childhood. But, as it was, with my lack of power, Oscar made me feel like the fly on my own porch. And there was no place else for me to go. It is difficult, to this day when driving home and turning from Highway 51 onto Highway N into home to control my fear."

Back home wiffle-ball was the game.

George and Charles called balls & strikes just like Jack Buck.

Prior to first grade, Oscar and I played together all day, everyday. He would walk by the house and whistle the signal to come out and play. We were great pals. But when school started, he wasn't allowed to play with me anymore. Mr. Oscar decided he didn't like my dad's politics, and he was successful at passing his scorn on to Oscar. Instead of walking by the house to whistle for me, Oscar now started walking around the ball diamond to avoid me. At school, he would lower his voice when I was around and watch me out of the corner of his eye, as if talking about me. For the next twelve years, he became a master at ridiculing and discouraging me. The more he mocked, the more awkward I became, until I was such a tangled up social mess it was no wonder people avoided me.

A daily trip to the local store was one of my chores. I dreaded it every day, but tried to hide my fear with a callous swagger. The local store was the community center, a place where people congregated, swapped stories, and told tales. It was a place to meet friends and be accepted. But when I would arrive, all the kids stopped talking. No one would include me. The statement was clear. "We don't want you." Maybe the most painful part was that I could never figure out why. Everybody always seemed to know something I didn't.

If my home town had been a larger community, I could have found a different group to join. But in our small town there was only one group. It was that or nothing, if you wanted to belong at all. Friendship with those out of the group eliminated all chances of acceptance, so no one was willing to break with the group to befriend me. I was the leper. Oscar's poison had reached into every part of our small community. Even deep into my spirit.

At 17, the hurt was greater than family comfort. It was too sensitive to be touched. Healing can only happen with touch, but I was too hurt for that kind of vulnerability. In the face of such painful, relentless, and bewildering rejection, I came to believe I was crazy.

Little did I know that I was born bi-polar and even reality was viewed through a hazy cloud. It was hard to distinguish between abuse, depression, and reality. The future could hold no wife for someone like me. Why inflict my pain on another, or create another life, only to suffer similar madness?

My brain was surely insane, interrupted by occasional moments of sanity. And I was so demoralized, I ouldn't tell the difference. Whether sane or insane, I had a few much needed distractions from the pain. During the seventh grade, the principal was the teacher. Another school district was merging with our school district, so new students were arriving to join us that day. And in walked the most beautiful girl I'd ever seen. Actually, she was the only girl I'd truly seen to that point. All other girls had just been one of the guys. Life is filled with pain, but beauty heals pain. My certainty that I could never pursue the comforts of a female vanished. When she walked in, I stood up. She walked to her seat and I followed, jaw slack. She turned around and said, "I'm Cynthia."

I replied, "I'm in love." My hormones had discovered the light. I realized there was no such thing as life before puberty.

Another distraction from the pain was my brother, Charles. Every evening we'd play whiffle ball. We never had a home plate. The grass was worn off both sides, so we just guessed at balls and strikes. In accordance with my rules, I always won. If not honestly, I'd cheat. He expected it. On the first base side of the field was a huge mulberry tree. Charlie hit left-handed, so we made a rule that anything hit in the tree was a double. Third base was wide open and I hit right-handed. Fly balls to left field were home runs. Other special rules were:

1) Anything over the brooder house was an automatic grand slam. (Of course, brooder house was 3rd base line).
2) Anything hit into the cattle trough was an automatic win.

3) Anything hit through the chicken house door was a grand slam.
4) Foul balls were out.
5) Anything caught rolling was an out. (A pop fly, caught, even with no one on base, was a double play.)
6) The pitcher called strikes and balls.

Any other rules could be added as I saw fit. Whiffle ball was the icing part of life—pure joy. And adding to the joy was calling the game in the voices of Harry Carey and Jack Buck.

A few years ago, my brother gave me a dozen whiffle balls for Christmas. This was his best gift. I recently gave him a home plate made of real wood and painted white. It didn't cost anything, but it packs a whole childhood of joy. And it's something he can enjoy with his son, Merry Christmas, Charlie.

When a new girl, Barbara, came to school, she received the same rejection as me. After a few months of watching her tormented the class cruelty turned my stomach. Class was ready to begin, but the teacher hadn't arrived. In the close presence of our newcomer, four boys, including Oscar, started making foul remarks. They were "real men," and they apparently didn't want Barbara to miss that fact. But I didn't think any girl deserved such disrespect.

I turned around and looked Barbara in the eye. She was hearing every word they said. Oscar was the prime offender so I slugged him in the mouth. I was raring for more, but other students held us back. The principal at that time was J.C. Wagner. When the principal was called into the situation, he didn't even ask me what happened. He just said, "What took you so long?"

It would take more than one fist fight to settle my score with Oscar. During a basketball game junior year, I was open on a fast break and not one player, including Oscar, would pass me the ball.

It seemed they'd rather not score two points than allow me a basket. So, I quit the basketball team. It was such a pity; I had given Oscar control of my own fate. Now I was an outsider, even from the game I loved.

Enraged by this last straw of social thievery, I took my twelve gauge shotgun, went to the gym, pulled back the hammer, and ighted on Oscar. But I couldn't pull the trigger. To pull the trigger would ruin my family name and would be contrary to my Catholic upbringing. A moral fiber held me back. I walked out to Flint Rock Hill and sat down to cry. I didn't know the name of what I was going through, rejection. For me, life was a game that had no understandable rules. There was no point in trying. The only thing I could do was harden my heart so it didn't hurt so much.

Right then and there, I planned my strategy. I would join the Marine Corps, learn how to pull a trigger on a man, and come back. Someday I would get even.On May 30th, 1966, our small town graduated the largest class in its history—21 students. Twenty went to Florida; I went to San Diego. My reception was firm, "Stand on the yellow feet." Boot Camp gave me a new parent who was big and strong. His speech told me I was not in the Boy Scouts and he didn't care about boyhood pain.

The command to stand on the yellow feet is the most horrific command ever given a civilian. The Drill Instructor grabs you by the shirt while shouting something about your mother and demands you place your feet on the deck where yellow feet were painted. From there the new recruits are herded like cattle to the barber and on to get their uniforms. Standing on the yellow feet is the transition from civilian life to life in the military. Forty years later, I am standing on the sun bleached yellow feet remembering my night of birth into becoming a maggot. From there, I would be become a member of "The Few the Proud, the Marines."

GEORGE P. HUTCHINGS - COMBAT SURVIVAL

Standing on the Yellow Feet painted on the pavement is part of boot camp training for new recruits. Years later George returned to the Marine base and stood on the same yellow feet, remenbering hls transition from civilian to military life.

GEORGE P. HUTCHINGS - COMBAT SURVIVAL

Firing range, 1966, Camp Pendleton, California
George fires expert at firing range.

George visited Camp Horno 40 years later and remembers the
steep hills he ran with a full pack.

GEORGE P. HUTCHINGS - COMBAT SURVIVAL

CHAPTER 4
FROM HELL TO THE
ETERNAL INFERNO

A Marine spends 90 days in a hell called Boot Camp. The promise of leaving boot camp and entering our first duty kept us alive. No one could spend their life in Boot Camp, so we looked to the future for easier times. Those easier times was called, Duty, the reprieve from our present hell.

But it didn't happen that way, after boot camp, Camp Horno and the reconnaissance battalion awaited me. Training here was Nam training and made boot camp seem like the boy scouts. Camp Horno was surrounded by mountains, desert wilderness, and heavily wooded areas. The morning chant started something like this:

"Up in the morning, before the Sun (04:00),
On the street for our morning run,
One, two, three, four we love the Marine Corps."
Five, six, seven, eight, we hate porky bait (candy).

There was more to the chant but cannot be mentioned in polite company. And up the mile high hill behind the barracks we went. We ran the hills day and night. The only difference between Boot Camp and Recon was Saturday and Sunday. Saturday and Sunday were ours.

After three months of reconnaissance training we could chose our next duty station. Japan was open! Wow, I didn't have to go to Nam. I had always wanted to go to Japan because they had the most beautiful women in the world. Japan would be my new heaven.

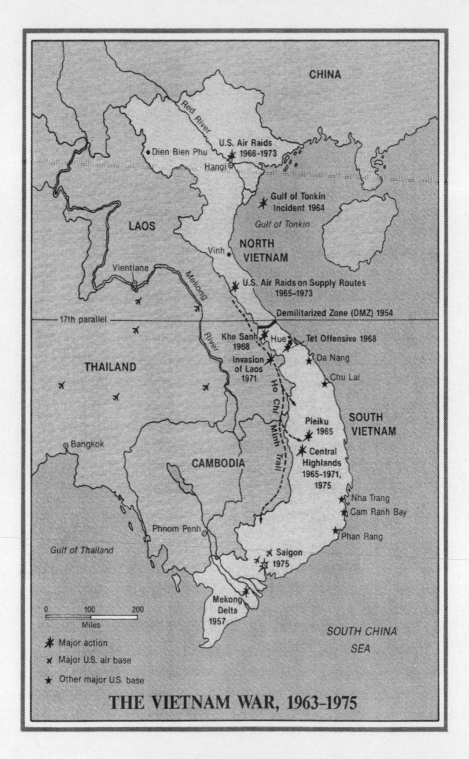

CHINA

• Dien Bien Phu

Red River

U.S. Air Raids
1966–1973

Hanoi

Gulf of Tonkin
Incident 1964

Gulf of Tonkin

LAOS

Vinh

NORTH
VIETNAM

Vientiane

Mekong

U.S. Air Raids on Supply Routes
1965–1973

Demilitarized Zone (DMZ) 1954

17th parallel

River

Khe Sanh
1968

Hue

Tet Offensive 1968

THAILAND

Invasion
of Laos
1971

Da Nang

Chu Lai

Ho Chi Minh Trail

Pleiku
1965

SOUTH
VIETNAM

Bangkok

CAMBODIA

Central
Highlands
1965–1971,
1975

Nha Trang
Cam Ranh Bay

Phnom Penh

Phan Rang

Gulf of Thailand

Saigon
1975

Mekong
Delta
1957

*SOUTH CHINA
SEA*

0   100   200
Miles

✳ Major action

✕ Major U.S. air base

★ Other major U.S. base

THE VIETNAM WAR, 1963–1975

No more night times maneuvers and screaming sergeants. My wish came true, on January 27, 1967, I reported to the Atsugi Naval Air Base.

My duty was to guard the front gate. Each vehicle was to be checked. But nobody told me why or for what. Vehicles were assigned stickers that would allow automatic passage but no one showed me a sticker. I was doing a good job letting any and all vehicles through the front gate. Then a Japanese dignitary backed up and told me he wasn't supposed to enter the camp unescorted. Maybe I shouldn't be there unsupervised?

Some guard I was! I was living in a country I knew nothing about, moving into a barracks full of a people I knew nothing about— blacks. It was a pity no one had warned me about culture shock; Dad just said, "Be flexible." A kid from Southeast Missouri, I had never met a black man in my life—except for Bob Gibson and Bill White, baseball heroes with the St. Louis Cardinals. Bollinger County, Missouri, didn't have a single black family. But Dad had taught me not to prejudge people, so everything was okay, right?

Wall lockers divided our barracks into living (or dying?) cubicles. All three guys in my cubicle were black. They spoke a different language, walked a different walk, and their handshake was very strange. It wasn't that I didn't like them; I just needed time to adjust to their culture. But they weren't inclined to give me that kind of time, and they sure didn't care to waste time on my acquaintance.

They decided to skip the courtship, and take an immediate and great offense to me. It was the same miserable song and dance of rejection of high school, same song second verse. Instead of "home sweet home", my cubicle felt more like East St. Louis, where throats were cut cheap. Not long after arriving, I was issued a new ammo belt and I put a "#" identifying mark on the inside portion.

Marines trained for combat and to give aid to civilians.

One day, upon my return from the head, the belt was gone, but, lo and behold, one of my cubicle mates had acquired a brand new one. That evening, when no one was around, I inspected his new belt; the # sign was there. I called the Sergeant, and the belt was returned.

That may not have been the wisest move for a naive, small town white boy to make. If I had any doubts before, I didn't now. I was certain the three of them wanted to take me out and cut me wide, deep, and frequently. Late one night they came in drunk and loud. One of them pulled out a bayonet. But the sergeant heard the disturbance and came in to break it up.

My first opportunity to "be flexible" certainly hadn't turned out to be a public relations success. From then on, it was difficult for me to sleep.

GEORGE P. HUTCHINGS - COMBAT SURVIVAL

Japan was full of firsts: First foreign country, first black "comrades", and first indulgence in drinking. With no desire to spend time in my cubicle, and an enlisted men's club near by, I chose to keep long company with Mr. Tom Collins. One day, I was supposed to help bring the flag down at 1700 hours (5:00 PM). Mr. Collins forgot to remind me of the time, and I missed the duty. The Sergeant chewed me up and spit me out, but nothing went on report.

By that time I had proven to be such a poor guard at the gate, I was switched to the night watch, guarding a fenced-in water tower. My weapon was an empty .45. Not only was the gun empty, I wasn't given any bullets. Barney Fife got more respect. Some company was provided, however—Miss Loretta Lynn. Over and over, all night long, she sang Don't Come Home a Drinkin' with Lovin' on Your Mind. This wasn't a "new heaven"; it was purgatory! Miss Loretta and the threats of my cubicle comrades got the best of me that night.

After duty, I got tanked up and threw myself in front of an automobile. The driver, who turned out to be the camp commander, swerved, but continued on his way. He ordered that I be found and taken to the hospital. But before they determined who the suicidal soldier was, I was back at the barracks, afraid to enter my cubicle. Still tanked, I knocked the sergeant down, took the .45 caliber pistol and put it to my head. Unfortunately, he was like me—no bullets.

I was taken to a mental ward where I was supposed to vent my nervous energy and depressurize by playing basketball. But it wasn't that easy for me. After one game failed to succeed at "venting my nervous energy," I got a broom and broke off the end to form a weapon. The security guards picked up a mattress and pressed me to the wall. They gave me a shot of something, put me in some kind of wire cage, and I woke up in a padded cell.

In 1966 the term bi-polar was not yet discovered. But I was suffering from the low end of a bi-polar condition. No one knew how to help. Alfred Hitchcock made a movie called Psycho. In the movie, the killer is in prison when a fly lands on his nose. He thinks, "See, I wouldn't even harm a fly." I did the same thing. I would convince myself I was harmless, the stewards would let me out, then the slightest incident would fill me with self-hatred again, and I would revert back to rage and suicidal actions. The doctors could bind my hands and feet, but they couldn't loosen the bondage of my embittered spirit.

I had come into the Marines to dump a past of rejection and isolation, only to discover I had bought into a whole new load of the same pain. I was compressed on all sides by the rejection of past, present, and a certain future of more of the same. Mental pain without any room to cope was driving me over the edge.

A fellow Marine told my shrink he had heard me say I wanted Blood—that I wanted to go to Vietnam. When the doctor questioned me about this, my first thoughts were, "I can save myself the suicide or dying in the cubical by going to Vietnam and dying with honor." Here I constantly faced fear that was demoralizing my spirit: the psychological death of rejection and physical fear of death at the hand of fellow Marines.

At least the fear in Vietnam would be manlier. Death in Nam under an enemy's hand had honor; death by a Marine knife in my own barracks did not. It seemed easier to die than to live this way. This was the heroic patriotism that led me to volunteer for a tour in Nam. The motive was mixed, I wanted to fight the Communist and protect my nation just as my father had served honorably in World War II. But I didn't want to die in my own cubical.

It seems strange that a doctor in a mental ward would let a suicidal patient volunteer for Nam. But the only statement I remember from my stay in the hospital came from him: "Remember the hounds of heaven." Before the hunt was over, I was to become well acquainted with them. But for now, the only thing I knew was that this "new battle for survival." was over.

First duty had come and gone. Nam was next on the roster of miseries and white or black would be no issue there. Charlie (our nickname for the Communist) was the entire enemy, black and whites we need each other.

Operation Medina - We had walked into an enemy force 3 times our size. After we ran out of ammunition, Captain Ruffer led three counter-attacks without ammunition, using entrenching tools and machetes. The last counter-attack we had nothing, so he began to sing the Marine Corps hymn, and we joined in. The enemy was confused and disappeared Into the jungle.

GEORGE P. HUTCHINGS - COMBAT SURVIVAL

Corporal Morgan Bice

CHAPTER 5
HIGH NOON

"Is this Charlie Company, First Platoon?" The replacement was laden with weapons of warfare and struggled as he battled the desert sand. "Yeah," I shot back. "You must be Charlie's new target." My sarcasm didn't faze him. He responded, "I'm behind you all the way!" This was a man I could like, and he became known as Bice.

An unassuming man, Bice was different from the rest and hard to figure out. He didn't use drugs, sometimes spoke about Christ, and carried his load like a man. He spoke of his girl friend back home with a gleam in his eye. When he spoke of her it was like he was lifted out of this God forsaken place. I liked to listen. He was in the first squad andI was in the third, so we seldom had opportunity to speak. When we did, though, I was glad he was on my side.

October 12, 1967, Bice and I were among the battalion waiting on the flight deck for helicopter pick-up. We didn't know where we were headed, but we knew it was to be a big search and destroy mission called Operation Medina. After what seemed like hours, the helicopters arrived and we headed for our destination, an unsecured, hilly field in the middle of the jungle. The edge of the field provided perfect cover for an enemy machine gun ambush.

Our choppers hovered about nine feet off the ground while we jumped. This maneuver could have been a Marine Corps blooper training film. It provided comic entertainment for any audience. The steep grade of the land, combined with the wind from the chopper blades and our awkward gear, forced us to roll in perfect Marine abandon all the way to the bottom of the hill. Charlie surely sat back and laughed-America's finest!

GEORGE P. HUTCHINGS - COMBAT SURVIVAL

1967 Marines waiting on the tarmac - Operation Media.

The camoflaged enemy at Medina.

Once on the ground, we were to trek into the jungle to our final destination. But we had one problem. Our fearless leader with the gold bar couldn't find an azimuth-a direction on a compass. He was a ninety-day wonder straight from Officer's Candidate School, a platoon second lieutenant with no experience. "Second Lieutenant" is often used as a title of ridicule and disrespect, and today we knew why. Charley Company was lost.

To be fair, I had never met the man and on this day even a Second Lieutenant deserved a break. The vegetation was called triple canopy jungle. The canopy was tall and dense. Our point man had climbed a tree, but could find no reference point. Now behind schedule, point man finally found a trail and radioed the lieutenant.

The question was, "Do we use the path or hack a new trail?" Our situation was critical. We needed to make up for lost time, or we would be forced to establish a make-shift defense for the night. We could make better time on the trail, but one of the rules in jungle warfare is, "Never take a trail," and everyone knew it. An invitation to a Charley Party is a trail. The hors d'oeuvres are usually tracers, followed by rockets, and Dracula for dessert. A twenty-three-year-old, completely inexperienced to our knowledge, the Second Lieutenant was making life and death decisions that included me and Bice. What I did not know was that the Second Lieutenant was taking orders from the Battalion Commander 20 miles away. The decision came, "Take the trail."

Before our point man hit the hundred-yard mark, we were ambushed from two sides. Thirteen men were killed in front of me and countless more behind me. I was in shock; never had I heard such noise or saw so many dead. Never-the-less I returned fire and my M-16 jammed. The information that Charlie Company had walked into an ambush of an enemy four times our size was not known until forty years later. This information was discovered while reading, "The Lions of Medina," by Doyle Glass.

GEORGE P. HUTCHINGS - COMBAT SURVIVAL

A Vietnam river crossing - easy targets.

Our group (we no longer had enough standing to be called a squad) was ordered to make a right turn and take the top of the hill. The intense jungle heat, the darkness of the canopy, the hill's steep incline, the drag of eighty pounds of gear, and the stark anticipation of imminent enemy ambush made the order a tall one. I was a Marine and I take orders. But this right turn turned out to be a better order than staying at the bottom.

As we inched up the hill the foliage became my worst enemy. I carried the radio and had pulled the tape measure style antenna pulled down so it would not tangle in the canopy. I would take a step and slide backward.

Again I tried and back I went. Minutes of fighting the incline and foliage seemed like an eternity. We needed to get to the top of the hill to protect the company from being flanked and surrounded.

GEORGE P. HUTCHINGS - COMBAT SURVIVAL

And I couldn't move two steps! Finally, the man ahead of me saw the problem. As I pulled the antenna forward it was folding over a tree branch. I was tangled. He corrected the problem and up we went.

It was now dark. It was the darkness I knew from being in a cypress swamp back in Bollinger County. No street lights, moon, or stars-total darkness, my hand could not be seen in front of my face. But I could hear the grunts of Marines in front of me and I followed those grunts. It was the music of determined men.

The resistance was light. We would sometimes hear grenades falling from the trees but we walked around them and up the hill. We accomplished our maneuver without further causalities.

How many of us were on top to the hill, I didn't know. But we had our most difficult order. Hold the hill. We were not even taking incoming. But we heard the fight at the bottom of the hill. To the man we wanted to join in the fight, but we were ordered to hold the hill. The tormented cries of familiar voices could be heard. We saw the green tracer bullets from the communist.

My mouth had dried and felt like cotton. I couldn't even spit. There was a moment that I had the sensation that I had died and gone to hell. It was not a vision only a passing sensation; I could hear the sounds of dying men crying for their mothers. There were the constant flashes of rifle muzzles and the blast of grenades. And I could not go to help.

Years later I learned that the Prophet Isaiah had written that, "Hell was a place of darkness where there was wailing and mashing of teeth." I had peeked into hell and the worst of it was that I could not go help. We had to wait for Delta Company to reinforce our ranks.

October 12, 1967, George's Marine Battalion on a jungle trail.
Trying to read a map in the jungle is almost impossible.

Atop that hill, the utter darkness, crushing heat, and noise of defeat were suffocating. The only disturbance in the absolute blackness was the searing machine gun flash, bursting flames in both directions below us, and the explosion of grenades, both testifying to our company's demise. We would soon be alone, on top of a jungle hill, surrounded by the enemy who knew the terrain.

That was the simple battle description from my position. Thanks to Doyle Glass, "Lions of Medina" later I would learn of the heroism that took place.

GEORGE P. HUTCHINGS - COMBAT SURVIVAL

The Marines were out of ammunition but mounted a counter attack. Fighting with entrenching tools and machetes they fought hand to hand. In the mist of the fight they would find an AK 47 of a killed enemy soldier and fire back.

A man wounded in his left hand was crying and hiding behind a tree. The remaining company was being over run. The Marine next to the injured man said, "If you want sympathy you will find it between shit and syphilis. The Marine picked up his rifle with his right hand and got back in the fight.

Someone, "Yelled corpsman up." The reply came, "I don't make house calls." Laughter erupted and the Marines stood to fight.

Three times Captain Jack Ruffer lead counter attacks. In battle as on the basketball court a person becomes a valuable player only when he determines to abandon himself and throw himself without regard to life or injury, completely into the battle. On the final counter attack all Captain Ruffer had to fight with was a Hymn; He stood and began to sing: "From the Shores of Montezuma to the Shores of Tripoli." The remaining Marines thought he was crazy but then another Marine joined in, and the soft baritone song became a choir of men who had decided that if they were to die, they would die fighting. Marines abandoned themselves and joined in the song. "We fight our country's battles, in the air, on land and sea."

The decision was simple, they could stay there and die or stand and fight with the only weapon available, courage. The Marines gathered their courage into song and stood to fight singing the next stanza "First to fight for Right and Freedom and to keep our honor clean, we are proud to claim the title of United States Marines." The enemy must have thought these Marines are crazy, but the enemy fell back allowing time for Delta Company to arrive. This information was a lost chapter until Doyle Glass spent five years researching all the survivors and wrote it down in his book "Lions of Medina."

GEORGE P. HUTCHINGS - COMBAT SURVIVAL

October 15, 1967, medi-vac removing wounded and dead.
A dangerous procedure, as choppers were an easy target.
The stench of blood hung in our nostrils.

At midnight all firing ceased. It was the black pre-dawn of a new day, Friday, the 13th. In keeping with new orders, we now stumbled down the hill, perfect targets, looking to join Delta Company. Approaching, someone from Delta hollered out,

"Who's there?"
"Charley Company," we answered.
"Who won the World Series?"

This kind of identifying dialogue was necessary, because Charlie could imitate American voices.

"Who has a newspaper?"

GEORGE P. HUTCHINGS - COMBAT SURVIVAL

Beautiful words came back, "Jack Buck just announced that, 'The Saint Louis Cardinals and won the series.'"

I asked, "Where have you been?"

A boy from Southeast Missouri who would turn eighteen in nine days there could have been given no better birthday present. In another part of this same world, under the same sky, the Saint Louis Cardinals were still playing baseball games. And they were winning.

"Come on in!" was the invitation. I found myself along side Bice. We were dying of thirst. I knew how many rounds I had left and I knew what I had in my pack, a can of peaches. I took off my pack and fumbled for a can of liquid. My, John Wayne or P38 (can opener) hung around my neck. Bice heard the can being opened and asked, "What's you got, peaches?" With a smile on my face, I drank the sweet nectar and handed it to Bice. The syrup was thick with sugar, but it was wet. Afterwards, we went back up the hill to dig in for the night. Digging a hole when you can't see the ground is a good trick.

Though the rest of the night hours were still, the quiet was worse than the earlier battle. Dark silence gave time for thought, and fear gripped my mind. Another "jarhead" and I took turns sleeping and standing guard with grenades. If anything moved, we would have to throw a grenade because a muzzle flash gun would identify our position.

Sometime during the night it began to rain, and our scrabbled-out hole filled with water. In stark contrast to the jungle heat, the rain brought with it a relentless bone-curling cold. I urinated down my leg to get warm, but it didn't work.

A whole new change-up of problems came with the morning sun. The morning was quiet. No one wanted to talk or move but the light began to bring energy and we slowly crawled from our positions to see who was alive.

My orders again were to hold my position. At the pinnacle of the mountain I could hear choppers coming in to evacuate our wounded. We quietly scavenged our dead for ammo and rations. The bodies of our fallen were sacred and the taking of their things seemed a sacrilege. But we did not know when or if supplies would come.Friday the 13th came and went with Marines caring for the wounded and dead. The day was a holy day as we honored those who fell in battle. In silence we fought to keep our own souls.

Saturday, October 14th, our foxhole was full of water and needed to be bailed, but the Communist would surely hear us bailing. And getting out of the hole meant exposing ourselves to an enemy that might be just behind the jungle canopy ahead. We sat on the rear of the bunker, facing the front, with our feet dangling, like soaked sponges, in the wet foxhole.

With wet feet came the fear of jungle rot, a plague that infests a scratch, but quickly becomes a fungus, covering an entire foot, leg, or arm. The medic had no cure for jungle rot. The only thing we could do was try to keep our feet as dry as possible. So, at every chance I changed out wet socks for the reserve pair of dry ones kept packed in a plastic bag.

That morning I removed one boot, wrung out my sock, and then put on a dry sock. I only removed one boot at a time, in case of attack. While sitting there, one boot off, giving cover to my partner as he bailed out the water with his helmet, the captain came and ordered me to water detail.

I cursed about my orders and Bice said, "George, I'll go for you." Before I could reply, Bice took a group of men and departed. Just after he left, a sniper battle erupted. I was ordered to hold my position while Sgt. Livingston checked our perimeter.

In Japan, before coming to Vietnam, my first experience with blacks had been fought with serious problems.

On this day, Sgt. Livingston balanced the scale. Using the precision of skill and sharp instinct, he out-maneuvered the sniper who had slaughtered our company and shot him like a possum. When the sniper fell from his position in a tree, our side cheered like hounds.

By the time our perimeter was cleared, several hours had passed, and I went to check on Corporal Bice. I found him-head and boots. We knew his boots because they bore his signature. He had been hit in the chest with a light anti-tank weapon. My inner voice said, "He died for you; Christ died for you." An unseen hand was drawing me, but I had no idea how to link up. Turning to the jungle canopy I fired my M16 on full automatic until empty. Word came to me offering an evacuation. I said, "No! I'm here to fight; I just had to deliver notice."

It took three days to evacuate the wounded and the dead. And in those three days we became acquainted with another demon, Stench. Decayed blood, we were stunned by the smell of our own dead.

We also continued the evacuation of the wounded and dead. The rumor was that our Second Lieutenant was evacuated with heat exhaustion. In our mind he couldn't face his men. His dignity was now lost, and all who knew him on that mission would remember him as a coward.

He would no longer have a military career, but would hide in a sea of civilian faces hoping no one would remember Operation Medina.

The second lieutenant was evacuated with heat exhaustion. Bice was evacuated dead. Those evacuating us had the assumption that the rest of us were alive and unwounded. They were wrong.

This Marine is being lowered into a hot landing zone
to take out the wounded.

GEORGE P. HUTCHINGS - COMBAT SURVIVAL

Doyle Glass has become a twenty-first century hero. His five year in-depth research into Operation Medina exonerated the Second Lieutenant who I had loathed for forty years. To The Lieutenant and all those of Charlie Company, I can say that I am proud to have served with you. I wish I could have done more, but I held my position and followed my orders. I was a good Marine.

My times line is fuzzy. It was one of those nights on Medina when I was ordered to go to the bottom of the hill with two other Marines. We were to provide a listening post. I didn't want to go. Walking down that triple canopy jungle would wake every dead Viet Cong. But we went, and when we go to the bottom of the hill undetected in unison we seemed to take one deep breath.

There was a voice on the other end of the radio, but I didn't want to talk. What did they want me to do just shout, "Here I am, come shoot me!" I keyed the hand set and held the hand set tight to my ear.

In the middle of this dark jungle, I thought I had the edge. We did not have to move any further and back in Bollinger County, Missouri I had spent such times listening for squirrels. I thought I could hear anything coming before it hit. But nothing moved, I removed my pack and reached for something liquid. But there were no peaches to quench our thirst.

The command came to come back in. I spoke, "No one is shooting at us, let us stay the night." The command was repeated. I said, "I don't want to." Then there was that famous Marine sentence, "That's an order." And up the hill we went.

Thanks to information provided by Company Commander Captain Bill Major the following is a short list of the men I knew. "There, but for the grace of God, we could have all died," Bill Major, Marines of Charlie Company 1st Squad killed-in-action (KIA).

GEORGE P. HUTCHINGS - COMBAT SURVIVAL

12 October
Sgt Salvador Bazulto, USMC
PFC William Stanton Blessing, USMC
PFC Gerald John Brothers, USMC
LCpl Kevin Arthur Cahill, USMC
PFC John James Castillo, USMC
PFC James Michael De Abre, USMC
Cpl John Raymond Lee, USMC
Cpl William Thomas Perkins, Jr., USMC
PFC Roger Edwin Walton, USMC

14 October
Pvt Oliver Bell, USMC
Cpl Quinton Morgan Bice, USMC
http://www.usmcfew.com/0311/inmemoriam/
Semper Fi,
Jack Ruffer Company Commander

The Walk Out - The operation was canceled and we had to make our way back to battalion headquarters. The same path out was the fastest but also the most dangerous. We marched laden with extra equipment such as M79 grenade launcher rounds in bandoliers that cut through our shoulder muscles. We carried motor rounds, and belts of M60 machine gun ammo. Some of the men discarded the gear only to have it picked up and returned to them.

We reached a gravel road that I thought was highway one. The heat must have been 110 degrees. The road seemed to have no end and men fell out and had to be evacuated. After marching all day we saw the battalion headquarters.

The chow hall was in sight. We had beards filled with filth, smelled like the dead, and we did not take to standing in line, we stormed the chow hall.

Everyone got out of the way and we filled ourselves with fried chicken, corn, mashed potatoes and gravy. And immediately after we all came down with dysentery. Our bodies were no longer accustomed to good food, we desired C rations.

This hill was once triple canopy jungle. The picture was taken by combat journalist Mike Leahy after the landing zone was cleared. These Marines are exhausted, but still ready to fight.

A typical rice paddy crossing - always bogging down troops.

CHAPTER 6
SCORPION'S STING

The most dreaded duty in Vietnam, the most hazardous duty-the duty nobody Wanted was Scorpion, so named because it was a night-time stinger. A Scorpion squad of about twelve men set out after dark to be an outpost. Their job was to preempt a surprise attack on major forces. The Scorpion sacrificed A Few Good Men to give the main unlt advance warning of attack. It was considered a calculated risk-the commander's calculation, our risk.

Getting to and from headquarters to the outpost position was Scorpion's most dangerous challenge. Movement out into the night was stupid. When a Scorpion unit set out at predictable hours, walking a path established by the enemy, everyone was free to observe. Those already waiting in the shadows could see every movement, but Scorpion, moving though the open, and still adjusting to the darkness, could not see what lurked in the canopy.

Because darkness blinded Scorpion, each trooper kept a hand on the shoulder of the man ahead of him, making the line a row of domino targets. But, if this contact was broken, the unit ended up split or someone was left behind. I once lost contact standing in a rice paddy that was as dark as a cypress swamp. Contact was broken when I paused to inspect a noise I heard from my right flank. When I turned back, I was alone. I couldn't move for fear of being detected.

Panic rose into my throat. I was certain my mother would have a funeral to arrange, and that my girlfriend would not be marrying me. But my squad returned. In spite of the fear, Scorpion became a game to some. How many times could Scorpion beat Charlie without being stung itself? The darkness could even seem to have an enticing quality.

GEORGE P. HUTCHINGS - COMBAT SURVIVAL

American troops coordinating with South Vietnamese.

Some began to request the duty. "Men love darkness rather than light." The great fear in Scorpion movement was seeing muzzle flash. Each step toward the dark was a gamble with life. Hearing gunfire meant a battle and possible survival. Muzzle flash meant death. In addition, the VC had probably mined the path Scorpion took, so the man in front risked one step after another, every step of the way. One man after another walked in the footsteps of the man in front. Not to walk in their safe steps meant exploring new ground and duplicating the risk of finding a booby trap.

We were set up just outside of town on a hill when my squad was assigned the Scorpion duty. Just after dark, we left, walked through town on a narrow path, and set up at a T-juncture overlooking a river. We held our breath until 2400 hours (midnight), when it was time to return to camp. We would rather have spent the night at our post than walk the dark path back to camp. But this was part of the gamble. The man who sees daylight wins!

A head count was made and we started back. Tail End Charley's job, the last man in the squad, was to secure the rear. Each man in line kept track of the man in front of him and the man behind.

That night, our Tail End Charley acknowledged the man in front and turned to check the rear. Seeing the next man back, he waved. Then, remembering there wasn't supposed to be anyone behind him, he opened fire. The enemy returned fire, and we took off, running toward company headquarters. They ran the other way. No one was hurt. It was our guess an ambush had been set up directly across the road from where we were posted that night. When we left, the enemy became confused and thought we were them, so they just fell in behind. It was a Scorpion adventure turned comedy. Under different circumstances, we might have all had a beer together.

The relief of having a Scorpion round finished didn't last long.

South Vietnamese fought on the side of the U.S. Marines.

Our squad was given orders to detach from the platoon and reinforce an ARVEN compound (South Vietnamese Regular Army), suspected of having enemy infiltration among the ranks. What was this? This place may have been called the Sand Dunes. A permanent Scorpion mission, where we served as ever-present bait for the enemy? There was only one road into the ARVEN compound. Even though one flank of the compound was bordered by a steep incline and a river, it had been overrun six times, each time through the front gate.

That's why an inside job was suspected. Because of the suspicion of infiltration, each bunker paired an American with a Vietnamese soldier-two men per bunker, all around the compound. My bunker faced the gate that had been run down six times. Taking turns sleeping (therefore putting my life in the hands of a man suspected of helping the enemy) didn't make much sense to me. I don't know when I slept, but it wasn't at night with my new friend. For the next several nights, the gate rattled and the outline of a man's shoulders could be seen. I shot this man every night for a week.

GEORGE P. HUTCHINGS - COMBAT SURVIVAL

One day we were ordered to do a road mine sweep. Everyone was careful to step in another's tracks. We had also learned by this time to suppress the instinct to run up and help a man if he stepped on a mine. Marines bunched up become clay pigeons for the second inevitable attack-either more mines or machine gun fire. This time, though, the entire length of road was found to be clear.

We loaded onto a troop truck to return to the compound, not knowing Charlie had planted a new crop of mines on the road we had just swept. Charlie was probably one of the civilians who had cheered for us as we passed by on our sweep. The explosion threw us like baseballs. I hit the top of a weeping willow tree and fell through its branches to the ground. We prepared for further attack, but there was none. Incredibly, no one was seriously hurt, but we had one dead truck. And we had been served notice; Charlie strikes at any time and anywhere. This is the Scorpion scare, made all the more vivid in the dark of the night.

Another truck loaded us to finish the trip back to camp. The compound sign was there filled with holes. The man in the dark I had been shooting every night was just a sign. By the time our turn at Scorpion came around, my panic button was spring loaded. All the VC had to do was watch our one-lane gate open on a moon-lit path. Tin cans rattled like an alarm clock when the gate opened, giving notice to the whole eastern hemisphere that we were coming. Our fear of the dreaded muzzle flash cranked up with each step. But we made it through the moonlit exposure into the darkness without incident.

How much courage could I expect out of the men on such a night? Living on constant guard at the compound, always wondering if the guy in the bunker alongside us was an enemy traitor had frayed our nerves. Now we were out past the limits of sane fear, into insanity. About 100 yards from camp, just inside the darkness, I made a decision.

We sandbagged the patrol, and lay in a ditch until time to go home. This became a common practice among us. It may sound cowardly, but when you're looking into the flash of an AK-47, it's better to be smart than brave.

War has no rules; the man who stays alive wins. In the beginning, thirteen eternal months stood between us and life. For the first seven months, risky brashness was just part of the drama. We knew we were doomed, so why fight it. But when you crossed the seven month marker, with only six months to go, you became a "short timer", and every day created hopeful pressure you might make it. The game became: avoid enemy contact.

Our stay at the compound was coming to an end when we ran our last patrol. My command of map reading at that time could be compared to that of a Second Lieutenant. The entire map looked like a giant rice paddy to me. Where was a reference point? Standard procedure, when lost, is to call in a Willie Peter (a white-phosphorus mortar round) to establish a reference point. The squad leader attempts to determine his map position and calls for the Willie Peter from about 100 yards away. If the round hits, you know where you are. If not, "There's trouble in River City." On that last patrol, we called for Willie Peter three times, but couldn't see or hear where any of them hit. There's nothing quite like that vacant feeling.

Here I was, an eighteen-year-old squad leader making decisions for twelve men. What if we were attacked and some of our men were hurt?

What was I supposed to say when I called for help? "Come on down to 34th and Vine. We need some Love Potion No. 9?"

How in heaven's name was I going to lead these men back? Searching for landmarks, we stumbled into a village not indicated on any map. Tidy, well-kept huts had no inhabitants, but posters in the native language were hanging all over the place. We took a few of them for souvenirs, and filled our canteens with beautiful spring water. We then headed for our compound, wherever that was.

About an hour had passed when we ran out of luck. Machine gun fire erupted. My dread had come true. We had wounded, and I didn't know where we were or what to do. Instinctively, the medic ran toward the wounded and the squad fell into place, by now accustomed to the drill. There were no orders given; men simply reacted. When the firing stopped, we discovered we were only 100 yards away from the compound.

Vietnam nationals interpreted our souvenir posters: "Mined Area. Keep Out." I had gotten the men lost and then meandered them through a mined area. This was never going to happen to me again. The next morning I requested a mail-order map course. Within a week I could tell north from south, and was working on east and west. Grateful and ashamed were the words of that day. Only gratitude had the power to endure the shame of walking men through a mined area. Only humor could cope with being an incompetent squad leader. Basic training had given me physical strength, but not knowledge.

The information had been given but I had such a fear of the sergeants and officers that my brain could not function. Now, I had discovered that the battlefield was a game of knowledge as well as brawn, and we learned the rules at Recon but experience became the great teacher.

CHAPTER 7
WHO'S THE ENEMY?

We fought two completely different types of troops-the South Viet Cong volunteer army (VC) and the North Vietnam Regular Army (NVA). Charlie from the South was an invisible enemy, but we came to know him well. He wore no uniform. He was a civilian. Good at digging tunnels, hiding weapons, and planting traps, his game was to wound, demoralize, and buy time.

Their famous booby traps were often planted in broad daylight, without any danger of reprisal. A sea of eyes provided them with all the warning system they needed. Once a point man tripped one of Charlie's mines, the VC opened fire, and battle was over as fast as it began. They got us in bunches because they knew we would run to help the point man and trip more mines. Or Charlie would fire his Browning Automatic Rifle (BAR) into the air, knowing we would give pursuit, and trip a trail of mines.

Charlie was happy with a wound. A wounded man sent home was as good as a kill. The sight and sound of Americans being wounded scared the hell out of U.S. troops, and Charlie knew it. In fact, a wound was better than a kill. The enemy did their homework; they knew Americans valued life. When we had wounded, Charlie knew we would go to their aid before pursuing the enemy. This tipped our hand, allowing Charlie to hit-and-run. By the time we had evacuated our wounded, the VC were long gone.

I was not shot that day, but booby traps demoralized me because there was no way to shoot back. The sight of Marines with the legs blown off demoralized me. Demoralized is the right word because had the enemy stood to fight there would be a win.

GEORGE P. HUTCHINGS - COMBAT SURVIVAL

George filling sand bags for the bunker.

The booby traps delivered notice that the V.C. could hit anytime and there was nothing we could do. The battle was a no win situation.

The Communist used land mines for troops and for vehicles. One such device was called a Bouncing Betty or Mary Poppins. It was rigged to pop up about chest-high. A grenade would explode, usually causing death.

GEORGE P. HUTCHINGS - COMBAT SURVIVAL

Pungie sticks, another Charlie toy, were pointed bamboo sticks planted in a hole and covered by straw or grass. These were designed to wound and delay us, but were also sometimes fatal. The North Vietnam Regular Army (NVA) was quite different.

The NVA were uniformed and well-armed, using mostly Chinese or Russian-made AK-47s. This weapon stirred the fear of God in us because it featured a banana clip holding 40 rounds and fired fully automatic. It could be thrown into a swamp, picked up, and fired again. By contrast, our M16 had a straight clip holding only 20 rounds, and couldn't have a single grain of sand in the chamber or it would misfire. It was also not a weapon suited for hand-to-hand combat.

The M-16, if needed with a bayonet was real trouble. The same forward thrust movement used with the bayonet caused the M16's plastic barrel cover to come off, leaving a burning hand on a hot barrel. So, our philosophy was, if you're close enough to stick 'em, you're close enough to shoot 'em. The AK-47 was a solid piece of equipment; the M16 was a toy.

The army from the North was equipped, trained, and fierce. They often charged our position while high on opium. A friend of mine once had to shoot a man six times before he fell. When the NVA hit, it was definitely not Charlie's hit-and-run style. They were there to fight, usually forming an L-shaped ambush. Hitting us from two directions gave them the benefit of surprise and initial victory.

The NVA was a worthy opponent, equipped with mortars and sometimes even anti-tank weapons. Due to American firepower the NVA would hit and then disappear into the jungle. One day we were in battalion strength, on line with squads, when we came into the sights of a well-entrenched VC sniper using an American-made Browning Automatic Rifle (BAR).

South Vietnamese troops search out village huts.

This bipod-mounted machine gun with a 20-round clip had an unmistakable signature sound. (The United States had replaced it with the M60, a tripod-mounted 100-round belt-fed system.) When the sniper first opened fire, we retaliated, and ordered in motar backup-60 Millimeter Mortars. Radio slang for these was Mike Mikes. After the Mikes Mikes retaliation, my squad was given orders to approach and determine the sniper's status.

The sniper had been firing from a wooded area on the opposite side of a creek. We moved in that direction on line, not knowing exactly where he was, through a field of knee-high grass. Half-way there, the sniper opened fire again. We hit the deck, returning fire, making a lot of noise shooting into the brush and trees, and then we pulled back calling in 80 Mike Mikes.

GEORGE P. HUTCHINGS - COMBAT SURVIVAL

An 80 MM makes a big explosion. After the 80 MM barrage, our squad was ordered to approach again, halfway across the field-rat-a-tat-tat. Once again we fired blindly, and then pulled back. The funny thing about this scenario the Marines hit the deck and all fired their M16's on full automatic and all ran out of ammo at the same time. This was followed with silence as Marines retrieved another clip of ammo.

This time we called in 105's. A 105 is huge howitzer cannon. It looked like the whole place blew up! We approached again. Half way there . . . you know the story. This guy must have had a tunnel going back to China! We retreated 300 yards and called in 155's, the largest artillery available to our unit. From ten miles away, we heard what sounded like a freight train approaching. "Please don't be short," was our prayer. Faces were buried in the sand when the barrage hit. Scrap metal landed all around us.

"Golly, Moses, I'm glad that was our gunner." We approached again, and this time we were able to get all the way up to the creek without resistance. We could see that the sniper had been using a fallen tree as a bridge, and radioed this back to the captain. "Blow up the bridge," was the order." Great, I thought. "Whoever goes out on that fallen tree is dead. I was the squad leader and need to lead by example. I could not send one of my men to certain death, I took the walk."

An M60 was positioned to give cover fire for the man who ventured out to the bridge, our squad then moved on line by the creek. I went out to place C4 plastic explosive on the fallen tree and backed away, alive. Today apparently wasn't the day for being "Killed in action". The explosion hit and we surveyed the damage, then backing away on line, in the ready position. Just as I turned around, a rat-a-tat lead cut the grass around my knees.

Famous picture of South Vietnamese fleeing from approaching North Vietnamese Communist troops.

A few moments earlier I was ready to die, but now I fought to live. Jump or duck-I didn't know. Neither did I yet know an ancient manuscript read: "Are there not ministering spirits, sent forth to minister for them who shall be heirs of salvation?" When people are taking their best shot, it's good to have a friend.

That day, 1,200 Marines were given orders to side-step one sniper. I don't know who was in charge, but they must have been thinking one man wasn't worth the loss of ten or fifteen others. Or perhaps they thought anyone escaping such a beating deserved another day. Respect is hard to earn. But that day we detoured around a sniper and went on our way. After our sniper encounter, we found a road, and headed, single-file, back toward home. These treks were not simple. We carried a lot of extra gear, including mortar rounds, M79 grenades, and belts of machine gun ammo. One guy said we even carried the corporate jet. Under the heat, distance, and load, it was a weary, almost surreal trip back. We were no longer heroic soldiers in a proud march, but rather a beaten down chain gang in a shackled shuffle. We had entered into a place where it seemed the pain of living was greater than the purposes of life. So, life didn't matter any more.

The Jews of German concentration camps suffered far more than we. How did they survive? There had to be a reasoning mind that overshadowed the pain. Some of our men had girlfriends or wives, and this thin strand of hope kept them alive. Those who were medics looked forward to positions of success once they were freed from the war. I, too, needed a purpose weighty enough to carry me, day after day, through this existence. I needed a resolve that would make me impervious to pain. As Victor Frankl expressed in Man's Search for Meaning, "Man's ultimate freedom is the right to choose his own attitude." The lessons of Philosophy 113 hadn't been learned yet, so I had to create my own philosophy.

American tanks did their job routing enemy stronghold.
The tanks were seldom seen, but always welcome. Snipers
littered the buildings, but tanks secured the area.

Before the day's forced march, I had decided the only way to maintain sanity was to embrace fate.

"You came here to fight or die." Dying here would give noble meaning to my life. But, as the days passed and I found the pressure of hope rising, I needed a back-up plan. "If you live, it will be to see the death of Oscar." Now I was fortified with purpose if I lived or if I died.

This double-edged death wish carried me through each day's labor. But, it was like feeding on garbage to stay alive. I knew nothing, yet, about the bread of life or the eternal water that quenched thirst. So, as carrion of the sky, I lived on nothing better than road kill. The misery of my hate philosophy could be felt killing me.

GEORGE P. HUTCHINGS - COMBAT SURVIVAL

On one moment I was determined to be an atheist, then there was no right or wrong, or heaven or hell. Two minutes later I found myself cursing. Who was I talking with? I'm not crazy, talking to myself. I knew I was talking to someone, it must be God. With my intuitive knowledge I testified against myself that I believed in God. How to know Him was unknown.

Without a higher calling, I had allowed the endless march to reduce me to an unthinking, uncaring machine, hauling a load. So, when one of my men dropped out with heat exhaustion, I didn't even call the commanding officer. I left him there for the Communist to savor. The entire squad filed past him and said nothing. We had regressed to the philosophy of boot camp marching, where there wasn't a morsel of compassion for anyone who fell out. If you fell out, you had to take care of yourself. This was completely contrary to our most basic value, Semper Fi. Never let your men bleed to death on the battle field. The CO was marching behind us, and he did what I should have done. He stopped and had the man evacuated by helicopter.

How many times could I screw up as a squad leader, and still have things work out? Charley Company, First Platoon, had been cursed with a squad leader who never, on the first try, did things right. I soothed my conscience with excuses. "The CO was given training for this. I got no preparation. My training was to be a private, not a corporal."

The truth is-there was no excuse. I had shown my depravity in the full view of myself and everyone else. If it makes any bit of difference, I still carry the scars. I said we fought two completely different types of enemy. I actually fought three. And the last and most dangerous was me.

GEORGE P. HUTCHINGS - COMBAT SURVIVAL

CHAPTER 8
MUD, MISSED OPPORTUNITY
& MOON SHINE

We went next to Con Tien, a hill on the Cambodian border. The men we relieved were having a drunken and excited party-not in the camp, but in the truck coming out. This wasn't a good omen. Why were they so happy to leave? What was in store for us? To orient us to our new home, we were given a brief tour of the place, each of us exiting the tour at our appointed bunkers. My waist-deep bunker, which faced north toward Cambodia, had wall to wall mud carpeting, four inches thick. Another nice amenity was the L-shaped sleeping area-six feet long, under ground, and padded with a two inch mattress of mud. Before our arrival the Communist had mortared the hill until there wasn't a single blade of grass remaining.

Bared of its foliage, the relentless monsoon season had turned this hill into a slippery molehill of mud. The only thing that kept us from sinking in up to our calves was the improvised boardwalks. There was some good news, though. It was my turn to go on R&R (Rest and Relaxation). Australia beckoned, with all the allure of a sensuous woman-no enemy and warm sun. Yes! But before my plane arrived; I came down with malaria and ended up spending my entire R&R in the hospital. After that, it was back to the unit. Same mud, same rain, but not the same men. The Communist had planned a little party in my absence and most of my squad had attended the reception.

Why was I taken out of harm's way? What were the chances I would not be with my unit that day? Was this divine providence? Had these circumstances been prearranged?

GEORGE P. HUTCHINGS - COMBAT SURVIVAL

Marines dug their bunkers and trenches defending the hill top.

In that rough-shod place, there were no accommodations for inner questions. There was nothing but a sprawl of mud. I could only hope that, if I took one day at a time, I would be given the opportunity to clean myself and go home.

A second chance at R&R in Australia, a long way from the mud and muck, finally came. My hotel room was a wonder. It had a bed and clean linens! Comfortable living, at last! I thought, until a machine gun woke me up one afternoon. The bottom of the bed provided my cover. The firing didn't cease, I army-crawled across the floor to investigate. I had taken cover from a construction crew using a jack hammer.

As part of R&R, peer pressure and a Marine's "reputation" demanded finding a woman and a bottle of booze, but my parents had instilled in me a moral fiber that said, "No." Even if I wanted to, being an awkward small-town kid, I didn't know the first thing about how to begin an encounter with a woman I'd never seen before. And it wasn't just any woman I wanted. I needed someone who would let me bear my soul-someone who could take the edge off of life and heal my wounds. I needed the balm of a healing passion, not just lust.

But, feeling the pressure of living up to Marine expectations, I bolstered my Marine courage and decided to find "a woman." The hotel clerk was getting off duty as I set out. We had established a passing friendship, so I asked him to point me in the right direction to find some booze and a woman, as if this was a common pastime for me. (I didn't give him the long list of my requirements-all about needing the right woman. I settled for the short list.)

He said, "I'll do better than that. I'll take you." We hit several bars, but the right woman didn't materialize. After checking out our latest pub, I turned back to my host; he was gone.

George digging his fox hole.

It took me three days to locate him. I got his phone number from the hotel, and called his wife. She didn't seem worried but told me he was in jail for being drunk and disorderly. She wasn't worried?

He had stepped outside the bar to relieve himself and was arrested. Once again I had missed the judgment of my peers. Frustrated by my thwarted efforts to find a woman, and with time now running out, I found myself walking the streets at 2 a.m., totally driven by the wrong part of my body. The battle of hormones versus the morally of a good woman was sliding toward the hormones. I needed relief. Remembering a line from My Fair Lady kept me hopeful. The line goes, "With a little bit of luck, when temptation comes, I'll give right in."

I stumbled into a bar, ordered a drink and waited for the giving in to start.Instead of being joined by the beautiful, soft blond of my dreams, a couple of soldier type buddies came up alongside me. One patted my back and the other one ordered a round of drinks. About that time I noticed there were no women in this place, and something did not feel right. Small town Missouri has yet to see its first homosexual. Vietnam introduced me to my first fire fights and Australia introduced me to my first gay. Though I was still naïve, I knew I didn't have the genes to appreciate this company. I left. It was not until twenty years later that I realized I had been in a gay bar!

Thoroughly over-stressed by this point, the next day I headed for the golf course. The course offered a nice, safe change. The distance from moral conflicts did me good. I met two good fellows on the course, joined their party, and knots of tension began to loosen. Afterwards, they invited me to their home to meet their sister and have supper. It was a great meal and great company. Their sister was a beautiful girl. I always wanted to see her again, but it was too late. R&R was over and it wasn't in the cards. Next time I would start at the golf course.

George in his bunker at Con Thien, before being shot of the can. When they fire on you, never let them see you sweat.

Though R&R was spent before I got the relief I desired, I returned to my bunker in the grips of another kind of "relief." Not being accustomed to good food, Montezuma got his revenge. I needed a head in the worst way. There it was, still at the crest of the hill. Not a nicely enclosed port-a-potty, but a naked stool. Was I going to drop my drawers for all to see while muttering Rodney Dangerfield's line, "I don't get no respect"?

Boot Camp has erased any notions of dignity. Anyone, given enough pain, will do anything. Up the boards I went newspaper in hand. Assuming the position, I heard the firing of a mortar. I thought, "Surely they couldn't want me. I'm just chump change." I figured the mortar was headed for the captain's bunker. Boom! It landed right where I suspected.

GEORGE P. HUTCHINGS - COMBAT SURVIVAL

"Bloop," again! Had they adjusted their fire? I had exactly seven seconds to get down. Boom! This one hit half way between the Captain's bunker and me. "Bloop, bloop, bloop." The worst was now obvious they wanted me. With all my years of rejection I finally found someone who wanted me. But I didn't want them! With my pants still around my ankles, I ran down the boards. Boom! I dove into the ground like it was chocolate pudding. And that cursed mud was my salvation. The rounds went under the surface and then exploded in the blanketing muck. I was covered in mud, rain and other stuff that wasn't pudding. It took a few minutes to become funny. The man in my bunker laughed. He couldn't tell what mud was and what wasn't. After a few hours of wearing it, everyone would know.

The Viet Cong weren't just after a kill that time; not that they wouldn't settle for one. They were after a demoralized spirit among our troops. When a man is robbed of his dignity, he has no more reason to fight. But youth has the elasticity to bounce back, however, and humor is a powerful coping mechanism. Still trembling from the fright, I began to laugh. The communist was saying, "We put you to open shame before your own troops." I stood up on the front of my bunker and shouted across the valley, "I hope you can smell what you shovel. If it's my butt you want, take a shot at this." I turned around and mooned 'em!

General Westmoreland addressing troops.

CHAPTER 9
THE IDES OF MARCH

It was March 1968, and my inner voice was speaking again: "You are going to be wounded, but you won't die." Thanks for the warning! When and what was going to happen to me now? The only scripture I knew at that time was "Beware the Ides of March."

Convinced March 15th was my day of doom, I decided to use every protection afforded me to cheat fate. The buttonholes in my camouflage helmet cover allowed me to insert branches to disguise the outline of our headgear. In light of my warning, I dressed my helmet like a bush. When walking in column (one man walking directly behind another), if the line stopped, you knew it was believed to be a safe area. So, normally, we would stand in place until movement resumed. Now that I was fate's precious target, every time we stopped, I crawled into a ditch, behind a dike, or just flat on the deck.

Tension and the anticipation of disaster cranked ever higher as March 15th approached. Time was out of control. The clock was running, and this game was for keeps. On March 13th, choppers lifted our battalion to the peninsula where Operation Ford was to begin, and dropped us straight into the ghoulish arms of a graveyard. Grim Reaper had tipped his hat. From the landing site, we formed squad columns in battalion strength and swept northwards.

Despite our foreboding entrance, the scenario for Operation Ford wasn't so bad. Terrain was level, temperature was comfortable, and (best of all) there were no rice paddies-only open field with occasional hedge rows. But what mystified us was the fact that there wasn't any water!

Marines were never taught or ordered to torture prisoners.

Wasn't a peninsula defined by surrounding water? Didn't anyone have a map? (It sounded good to ask for one, but if truth were known, neither the lieutenant nor I could have read one anyway.)

"Don't think," I told myself, "Just keep walking and trust fate to carry you through." And in this manner, the 15th came and went. On the 14th I stepped on a pungie stick. Luckily, it was old, and my arch was high. It went through the bottom of my boot and out the side-just a scare. Nothing further happened that day. It was simply business as usual. But I couldn't help noticing graves all over the place.

March 15th we were in battalion strength on line, with about 1,200 men in a horizontal line of squad columns. There were three men in front of me, the radio behind me, and then the rest of the squad. I prepared for the worst, but nothing happened. What a bust!

I was feeling a bit foolish. The branches came out of my helmet. It was time for a deep breath. The 16th and 17th passed easily, and the 18th rolled up in the same manner.

Then shots rang from the right rear. I hit the dirt. Was I shot? It didn't really feel like it. Remembering my training, I didn't look at the wound. If you look at your wound, you might go into shock. I felt my hip with my hand and it came back bloody. But I could wiggle my toes, so I knew I would walk again. I was better off than the two men who had been directly in front of me. They lay dead, as was the radio man who had been behind me.

The medic gave me a shot of morphine, then left to attend to others. I had wondered what it would feel like to be shot. Now I was shot and it wasn't so bad, because everything was numb. "If this is as bad as it gets, I can handle this." Gradually, my thoughts grasped the turn in fate. "The war is over for me. I'll be leaving in just a minute, guys, so goodbye and good luck." This was rather grandiose optimism.

We had been pinned down by the North Vietnamese Army, so the battle had just begun. Corporal Ed Gant, who had been ahead of me, walking point with a shotgun, was spared when the right flank was hit first. Now he crawled over to me to swap weapons. "If we get overrun, you'll need this," he said as he handed me the shotgun. Why he had a shotgun, I'll never know. Apparently, he was still carrying it from jungle maneuvers. Very powerful at short range, a shotgun is worthless after a hundred yards. He took cover again behind a grave, and then looked over to find his target. He was hit right between the eyes.

The enemy was scattered in a hedge row and wooded area straight ahead. Our lines of defense formed behind me. Guys kept yelling to see if I was alive, but I didn't respond.

The horrors of war.

The NVA could see my every movement and I wanted to be thought dead. If they saw me move, they would hit again. Lying there with no cover, a machine gun battle raged just over my helmet. I had on a flack jacket, like a bulletproof vest, with lead four-inches thick. It was designed to deflect mortar rounds and grenades, but not direct rifle fire. I was also heavily laden with personal gear, including an ammo belt, a canteen, a pack of food, a poncho, and other various war implements. Laying low wasn't easy with all this bulk of gear between me and the ground.

My swaggering farewell to the troops speech had changed to, "Oh, God, get me out of here and I'll live for you the rest of my life." I had feared death but found the choice to live. I fought to keep myself and anyone around me to live. I was no longer fighting for my nation, I was fighting to live.

GEORGE P. HUTCHINGS - COMBAT SURVIVAL

When our machine gun broke down, enemy fire turned, for a moment, in another direction. Corporal Roy Munson crawled from his cover and dragged me back. A vehicle that looked like a tank without the cannon came up from behind and I was loaded in.

Because the ground beneath us was mounded with grave after grave, the going was very rough. I screamed in pain, and the medic told the driver to slow down. But we had been informed the enemy had antitank weapons and we were in a vehicle that made a perfect target. I told the driver to go on; I'd rather suffer the ragged "speed bump" pain than risk certain death. I couldn't believe I was leaving my last Vietnam battlefield. I wished I could have left with some kind of honor.

I wished I had been brave or had been a hero. At best, I was at the wrong place but at the right time to claim my only medal, The Purple Heart. We fought battles with victory, saw death with honor, and held our head high in spite of the media back home.

The DaNang hospital became my graduation stage where I became the youngest man in America to receive a Ph.D. The General came by and placed a Purple Heart on my chest and that became my Ph.D. in slow ducking. Today my vehicle licenses plate reads, Purple Heart Ph.D. SD for slow ducking.

After graduation the Ph.D. in "slow-ducking" came in handy as I later went on the speaking circuit and I tongue-in-cheek say the al-Qaeda found me inspirational. They strapped bombs to themselves and then ducked slowly! Do you realize that of all the armies that have ever marched the earth, some soldiers have deserted, but the al-Qaeda never desert, they commit suicide!

One scholar wrote Islam takes the basest human passions - lust, greed and murder- and adds to it religious fervor.

Body bags were a farmiliar sight.

Do you realize that the Muslim doctrine did not come into existence until about 622 A.D. Mohammad was jealous because the Arabs did not have prophets and the Jews had many prophets; the Arabs had no priest, but the Jews had priests; the Arabs had no Messiah, but the Jews had a Messiah.

Mohammad went up into the mountain alone and came down saying he had seen Allah and Allah was God and Mohammad was his prophet. The Jews have four thousand years of Messianic history, the Arabs have none. The Jews and Christians have over 5,000 witnesses that saw the resurrected Christ. The Arabs do not have a history of God leaving Heaven, taking on the form of a man in order to reveal himself to man.

The Muslims have a god – an evil concept that allows them to hate Jews and Christians and murder without conscience. This hatred will never end. It began in Genesis chapter 16-17 with Abraham and Hagar the housemaid of Sarah.

GEORGE P. HUTCHINGS - COMBAT SURVIVAL

Sarah laughed because God promised Abraham a child when he was 100 years old and Sarah was 80. Sarah arranged Abraham to go in unto Hagar and conceive a son named Ishmael. Later, Sarah conceived and Isaac was born. Ishmael mocked Isaac and Sarah drove Hagar and Ishmael into the desert. God promised Hagar that Ishmael would be the father of a great nation but the two cousins were fighting because the Messiah would come through Isaac. Ishmael would live in the desert and become a "Wild Donkey." The Arabs and Jews have fought ever since.

The Iraq war is an extension of Ishmael and Isaac. Allah is the figure of an angry man's jealously - a concept of evil to plunder and kill Jews and Christians. What I would like to ask Muslim clerics is: If a man is as old as myself, what good would 72 virgins do for him? I couldn't handle one. Do the virgins come with Viagra? Where did Allah get all those virgins? Are these virgins the ugly women who could not get a husband on earth? How can I check with Allah to see if he has a sufficient inventory of virgins? It would be just my luck that at my coming he would be out of inventory. And what does Allah promise the women who commit suicide? A martyr is someone who is killed for their faith. Why do Muslim clerics not go first and lead the way? A suicide bomber is not a martyr, he is a murderer.

Jesus never asked his followers to commit suicide, he ask them to live returning evil with good. Jesus is willing to receive the Muslims but the Muslims want to destroy the very memory of Christ and push the Jews into the ocean and kill Americans because they represent civilization. The word civilization comes from Christianize.

What will I do when the Muslims come to shoot me? I will steal the 72 virgins from the man who killed me and turn them over to Jesus. I don't need 72 desert women. Mr. Bush, I am doing a great job, just keep me on the speaking circuit.

GEORGE P. HUTCHINGS - COMBAT SURVIVAL

Vietnam the Global Win! - Vietnam is often considered the war that America lost. We lost 58,000 lives while killing over one million of the enemy and we still left town with our heads down. It would be another generation until our victory was revealed. The American hero's of Vietnam did not loose - they brought a global win! In Vietnam American aviators depended on rockets to shoot down enemy air craft. Dog fights were a thing of the past, but when our F 4's when up against Russian MIG's we had to learn the Dog Fight - and "Top Gun" was formed. Today we have the best aviators and aircraft in the world.

War always spills over on the civilian population, but with American J bombs surgical strikes can be made on specific military targets. Our stealth bombers and fighters reduce the risk of our pilots being shot down. Fewer of our troops are killed, and fewer civilians are at risk.

In Vietnam the starlight scope was first used. It was the forerunner of night vision goggles. The starlight scope did not work very well, but the night vision goggles used in Iraq are used to spot the enemy miles away. In Vietnam we used the 50 caliber machine gun and it is still the prize weapon in Iraq. But we now have a weapon that fires grenades like a 50 caliber.

Body armor called flack jackets were used in Vietnam. The flack jacket was used to cover the torso and was about four inches thick. It was thick, heavy and awkward, and only deflected shrapnel metal. Today, total body armor is used in Iraq. When stepping on a mine, neither suit will protect you.

The M-60 Machine Gun was used in Vietnam. It fired belt fed ammo and was hard to carry. Today, the SAW, is used in Iraq. The weapon is canister fed and is called the SAW because it fires so fast it can cut down trees and shoot through cinder blocks. The SAW is carried in each squad while the M-60 was limited to one per four squads.

GEORGE P. HUTCHINGS - COMBAT SURVIVAL

Vietnam was a global win because when America goes to war fewer civilians are killed and our troops are better equipped. Who in Vietnam would guess that one day we would have drone aircraft that can fire a missile. Vietnam was a battle that America lost, but it was a war the globe won. The American victory did not take place until the Gulf War revealed all the weapons developed since Vietnam.

1969 war protestors confront the soldiers.

North Vietnamese Army colonel, Bui Tin, called the American "peace movement" essential to North Vietnamese victory: "Every day our leadership would listen to the world news over the radio at 9 a.m. to follow the growth of the American anti-war movement. Visits to Hanoi by people like Jane Fonda and former Attorney General Ramsey Clark and ministers gave us confidence that we should hold on in the face of battlefield reverses."

GEORGE P. HUTCHINGS - COMBAT SURVIVAL

Public relations picture 1970.
Over 58,000 American lives were lost taking over 1,000,000
enemy lives - yet politicians would not let us win a victory.

CHAPTER 10
GOING HOME

Da Nang was the first stop after the battlefield. It was a secure area, from most of the ravages of war, but still in Vietnam. The severity of my wound was unknown to me, so the possibility doctors could patch me up and send me back into action mounted a growing fear. A spinal tap was ordered and I held my breath for the results. When I heard the magic words, "Send him home," it was difficult to restrain the tears. The pressure of fear had been removed, and pain at its worst was over.

The C-141 is a military jet used for carrying cargo-boxes, crates, etc. This is what they were preparing for me. I was to be transported in one of the rope litters suspended from the ceiling. "First-class treatment," I thought. "Am I cattle, guns, or equipment?" It was insulting to be considered as such, but it didn't matter; I was going home.

All I recall after departure is landing. It was in Alaska, and when the back door opened, the cold air turned my compartment into a deep freeze. A nurse came from some place delivered an extra blanket. She had long, blonde hair - An American Angel. "This is heaven," I thought," No words were exchanged, and I never saw her again. But her random act of kindness allowed me to reach down for the courage to fight another day. Surely everything was going to be okay now.

Our next stop was Scott Air Force Base, not far from St. Louis. It was great being back in my own culture. A phone sat beside my bed and a steak sat on my lap. I asked how much this cost. They said, "No charge." The next day I was flown to Millington Naval

The Wall is holy ground.

Hospital, near Memphis, Tennessee. Where I was reading a Playboy book with one hand and pinching the nurse with the other. My battlefield prayer, well...

My sister, Mary, called from Oregon. We had never gotten along very well, but by calling she was making an effort. I wanted to meet her effort and relax our barriers, yet we spent most of that day in a long-distance fight. It was a good sign, however. My killer instinct was still there. The argument demonstrated life. I wasn't down for the count. In fact, I still had heart.

While at the hospital, doctors put a pin in my leg and put me in traction. My parents arrived, and the first thing my mother said was, "Why are you so dirty?"

GEORGE P. HUTCHINGS - COMBAT SURVIVAL

"Dirty?" I replied. "I've had two baths. This is the cleanest I've been in months!"

They asked the doctor for a prognosis, and were told I had been hit three times with machine gun fire, and had surface wounds from a mortar. All three rounds narrowly missed a major artery, and only one shot nicked my hip joint. A quarter inch either way would have killed or crippled, but an unseen hand had guided the bullets through a narrow corridor of safety. My doctor said all would be fine. Appreciation for something of real substance is difficult to express. "Thank you, God," doesn't have much punch. It left me empty.

When my girl arrived with her parents from Imperial, Missouri, they let her enter the room first. She had long, beautiful hair, and when she kissed me, my blood pressure soared! Debbie had written me several letters about "George of the Jungle." I thought she had made up this character for me because I'd been in the jungle. I discovered this was actually a cartoon character that swung on a vine and asked, "Who greased the grape vine?" I didn't know whether to laugh or cry; I'd rather be compared to a jackass than a monkey. Laughter won, but with some reservation.

After a few months of traction, I was placed in a body cast that reached from my armpits to my toes. I was on my feet again, and the situation demanded painting the town red! The NCO (Non Commissioned Officers) Club was nearby, and a girl, some beer, and a good time were always waiting there. I spotted a pretty young filly dying to dance. I asked, she accepted, and we danced the night away. I couldn't slow dance and I couldn't bounce from my knees. But the cast had a walking heel on the right foot, and by pushing off with my left foot, I could spin around, doing the twist. It had been to long since experiencing fun like this. It tasted good and created a desire for more.

For the moment I was able to screw the lid on recent history with "a twist." But it wouldn't last for long. There was a chasm between who I knew I was and who I was thought to be by those who welcomed me home as a hero. Their esteem and my reality mixed like oil and water. But for now, Debbie and "George of the Jungle", a night on the town and a steak in my lap, had made me laugh, and it felt good to be loved.

But storms of pain and rage were gathering force at the horizon and just beneath the twist.

CHAPTER 11
TWELVE-GAUGE REMEDY

Orvil Seiler, my brother's future father-in-law, drove the 150 miles to Memphis to get me. I was to go home to Missouri. His station wagon was needed to transport a man in a body cast. Two men picked me up like a 2 x 4 and loaded me through the vehicle trunk. In some ways, it was like loading into a time machine. My home town was a quiet community in 1950, the year Paul Hutchings moved his family there. It's still a quiet community, little changed. From city limits to city limits, it takes less than one minute to drive through town. A post office, a tavern, a general store, a church, and a school, that's all. One blacktop highway is the town. There are two gravel roads that head toward the Bollinger County rain forest.

Close to home, we passed Paul England's farm, where I got my first job. Paul didn't want to hire me because everyone thought I was too thin to buck hay bales. But he was in desperate need of help, so he hired me. We started work at 6 a.m. and quit each day at 5 P.M. One day the sky was full of storm clouds and hay still lay in the field. Most of the workers knocked off at quitting time and went into town to get tanked. Recognizing the desperation of this farmer's situation, I stayed until the job was finished around midnight.

We beat the rain. Paul paid two cents per bale, and my share was about ten dollars. From that time on, I never lacked for farm jobs. We also drove by Henry Nenninger's garage. Henry never replaced spark plugs; he fixed them! It was Henry who taught me how to fish for carp at Mingo Spillway. Every Sunday afternoon we made the 30-mile trip to Mingo, and he always told the same stories with the original excitement. Each time they got better.

As we entered town, we passed the Beussink home where I had played softball with Virgie and spent many days playing in the orchard. Passing the school, I was reminded of John David Nenninger and the time we broke into the science hall. We didn't want to break or vandalize anything. We just wanted to make Mr. Mac look foolish.

Mr. Mac was growing bean sprouts so we dug them up and replaced them with watermelon sprouts. Some people are fun to irritate; Mr. Mac was one of those people. John David and I had thought breaking into the school would be "Mission Impossible."

After our success, we felt bulletproof. A standardized test was forthcoming, and our teacher hadn't covered the material. We knew it, Mr. Ritter knew it, and he knew we knew. (Mt. Ritter was a great coach, but not much of a science teacher.) So, John David and I broke into the office, copied the answers, and left. We planned on missing some questions to avoid suspicion, and we were prepared to defend each correct answer. But, when it was announced that only two students received test grades above a "C", we knew who both students were. And the Inquisition wasn't long in coming. These were all fun memories.

But everyone has bad memories from childhood, too. You are expected to grow up and leave those behind, but I wasn't grown yet. In spite of a war, a wound, and a rescue, I still wasn't ready to leave behind the grudges of childhood. Perhaps the irresolution of a vague war had left me looking for a battle I could win. Perhaps the discovery, within days of returning home, that my girlfriend never really had been, or ever would be, my girl had left me looking to pick a fight.

In retrospect, even while in Vietnam I had known Debbie was not, in reality, my girl. That's why I had chosen other driving forces to see me through the days of war: If you die, you get to die a hero. But if you live, you get to go home and see Oscar die.

I had come home alive. And now, looking out from my back porch, I could see Oscar's house. The Marine Corps had taught me how to use explosives, and had cleared my mind of conscience. The Marines had taught me how to kill in a hundred different ways, but they hadn't given me a victory. They hadn't given me an enemy I could defeat. I had been tricked into killing the wrong man and had been left with no satisfaction. But I could get that satisfaction now. My inner voice said: "Kill him."

Every pain in me cried out for satisfaction, and a twelve gauge shotgun sure looked like the remedy. Blood had become cheap, and I was entitled to the blood that would expunge my pain. Life couldn't go on without death. I loaded the gun and looked out across the field, to the fence at its border. The fence would be my line of embarkation. If I could cross the field and the fence, there would be no point of return. I hobbled across the field to the barbed-wire fence. The house across the way was in clear view and held in contempt.

Rage flowed through my veins as I lifted the gun, by the barrel, and smashed its stock over the fence post. This was my favorite shotgun. It exploded like a round being fired, but the round was aimed at me, not at Oscar. A hurricane of hate and bitterness for Oscar still hung over me, but its roar was lost against the bigger roar of the hurricane inside of me-the fury of hatred for my own self. Once again I could not disgrace my family and once again the moral fiber taught by my church restrained my evil.

How could this inner pain of rejection and bitterness be emptied from my soul? There was no answer, but hatred was actively killing me not Oscar. I was a man who had given power over his life to a bully, and then allowed himself be consumed with empty revenge. I was nothing more than a puppet of emotions. And the tension between these two emotional hurricanes would continue to escalate until one or the other was bound to destroy me.

George and Becky's wedding, November 15, 1969.

GEORGE P. HUTCHINGS - COMBAT SURVIVAL

CHAPTER 12
LUST IN THE HEART

After "recovery time" in my home town, I was sent to limited duty at Paris Island, South Carolina. Folklore from San Diego had compared Paris Island to a snake-infested swamp. The swamp was never found, but I can verify that Paris Island is the sand fly capital of the world.

It was my job as a sergeant to administer Military Occupation Specialty (MOS) tests. The duty was very manageable, and I had something I had never experienced before-time and money.

"Gosh, it feels good having no one was standing over me."Reveling in my newfound liberties, one weekend I went to town looking for a companion. A pretty girl was standing by a sea wall looking out at the ocean. She seemed lonesome. I walked up to her and said, "Nice isn't it?" Walking away, she said, "Come back at 2:30 for the submarine races. It's a big deal. Lots of people show up." Always the naïve country boy, I foolishly anticipated the meeting. I showed up early. It seemed everyone found pleasure in my obvious stupidity. Even strangers found it easy to ridicule but this was different, I was teased by a beautiful woman!

I couldn't buck the rejection of childhood or the rejecters who were to be my comrades. Either victory would have sufficed, but I didn't have the empowerment to do either. The siren call of suicide began to beckon again, so I was sent to a hospital in Charleston. Life there was great. We made our beds in the morning and played golf all day. But in spite of the light duty and easy-going schedule, a low-grade depression continued to burn.

Shortly after returning from the hospital, I met a young lady named Pat in a Laundromat. She liked the way I played with her two young children, so she invited me to her house. Pat was married so I knew we didn't have a future, but for the brief acquaintance we got along great. Her kindness loosened the knots of hatred in my mind.

Pat and me may not have been in love, but it was the nearest I'd had known. And her kindness made me hungry for a woman who could be my own. A few months later, my father had a heart attack and the Red Cross rushed me home. They didn't know my dad. By the time I arrived, he was out of the hospital, pushing off any attempts to slow him down. He was still the principal in a neighboring town and one of his former students was getting married, so he asked me if I wanted to go along. I told him, No I don't want to go." Pop said, "Well there will be a lot of pretty girls there." I said, "Well, I think I'll go." Pop wanted me to ride with him, but I preferred to drive myself. I followed him to the neighboring town, and then down a one-lane dirt road into the back woods.

What a setting for a wedding-special effects and everything. Even a blind person could have told you the little church was flanked by a chicken coop to the right, and a hog pen to the left. The hog pen looked nasty, but the chicken coop had the greater stench. I pulled my brand new '69 Volkswagen Beetle into the clearing and stepped out of the car wearing my new sergeant stripes, my military cover with visor, and my spit-shined shoes. My brass was immaculate, and I strutted into the church with a Purple Heart hanging on my chest. I was one proud rooster. Even a blind person could have told you I was coming.

The waft of crowing testosterone was enough to bowl anyone over. Dad had made a good decision in inviting me. There were at least 50 eligible women at the wedding and I was the only strutting rooster. All the other boys were out playing war. The pendulum had finally swung my way.

GEORGE P. HUTCHINGS - COMBAT SURVIVAL

After the ceremony, the girls formed a reception line stretching out before me. Dad enjoyed playing Cupid and he didn't miss an arrow. He introduced me to Becky, and the great wolf began to howl! I could look no further; this was the gal I wanted to marry. Given our destiny, I couldn't just shake her hand like I'd been shaking everyone else's. So I walked up and kissed her!

She blushed all the way down to the floor. Becky stirred emotions I couldn't put into words until fifteen years later, when Jimmy Carter became president. He made himself famous by admitting to a deadly disease: "Lust in the Heart." No one ever gets married without a healthy dose. Standing around making small talk wasn't my idea of how to spend time with Becky. We needed to go someplace. "Becky, I'm about out of gas. Is there a station nearby?"

"Yes," she replied. "Go to the end of the road, and it's on the right." (Remember there was only one road, and it only went one way.)

"Well, I'm not from these parts. Come with me. I might get lost."

Being even more naïve than I was, she bought the story. I discovered later, she hadn't really needed "a story"; she wanted to go somewhere with me. (Who foxed whom?) Bouncing down the gravel road in my new car, new stripes, and Purple Heart, I had never been prouder.

Then Becky looked at me and said, "How long have you been in the highway patrol?"

I chose not to be offended. She felt too good on my arm.

"I'm not in the highway patrol," I declared. "I'm in the service!"

"Oh," she said. "I never could tell those Army uniforms apart."

In spite of the double insults, we made a date for the following night. A little shy, and somewhat nervous, I calmed down with a few beers and went to pick her up. I took her by the right hand and my whole right side sobered up. This was a girl who didn't drink. We dated for the remainder of my leave, and believing this to be an extraordinarily generous courtship, before I left I asked her to marry me. She said no. "Why not," I asked?

"I'm not going to marry anyone with short hair, anyone in the military, or anyone under twenty-one." Throughout the rest of my stay at Paris Island, South Carolina, I drove to Becky's town every other weekend, on payday. The drive was 931 miles one way (if I didn't get lost in Nashville.) I got off duty at 17:00 hours (5:00 p.m.) and drove all night, arriving at 06:00 Saturday morning. I'd bang on the front door and Becky's mother would answer with a growl and put me on the sofa. Then we'd all get up at 09:00 and head for Cape Girardeau for the only form of entertainment available to us, shopping. The problem was, neither of us had any extra money, so we just looked. Then we would eat supper out and go home. I had to leave the next morning by 11:00 to report back at work by 04:00 on Monday morning.

Two places I always enjoyed seeing on those flying commutes were Kentucky Lake, with all the swimming pools and boats, and the Smokey Mountains. The speedometer on my '69 Volkswagen registered 90 M.P.H., but I could do 105 coming out of Lookout Mountain. It seemed like every time I went through there, the radio station would play Johnny River's Mountain of Love, and my heart pounded.

As soon as I could, I turned twenty-one, got out of the Marines, and grew some hair. Then I asked Becky again to marry me, and this time she said, "Yes." I'm not sure who won the negotiation, but it didn't matter. Good-bye Paris Island; hello Becky!

CHAPTER 13
A PRENUPTIAL AGREEMENT

Becky and I may have been ready to get married, but no one was ready to perform the ceremony. We first went to my parish priest to book the wedding. He informed us that since Becky wasn't Catholic, she would have to take instruction to become a church member. Never one to yield authority without good reason, Becky asked him if he knew for sure he was going to heaven. This is not the question I wanted to hear her posing the priest with whom I trusted my soul. (Or maybe it was the question I wanted to ask.) Of course, he was going to heaven! He was the priest, for Pete's sake! But he calmly and matter-of-factly replied, "No one can know that." Becky said, "I do." And his bid for authority with Becky had just ended.

I began to smell rotten fish. I had been following someone all this time who didn't know where he was going. Becky knew something he didn't. I should follow her, not him! But, in the end, my indoctrination won out. He was the priest and I was a peon. Becky wouldn't convert, but I didn't care about that. I could give her lovely mind and body all the space she needed for convictions. But, in the meantime, who would perform our wedding?

Becky suggested her preacher, Warren James. I agreed. A ceremony was a ceremony. This time it was my turn to be examined "in the faith." "Are you going to heaven?" her pastor grilled me. I was ready to tell him whatever he wanted to hear. "Sure, I'm a Christian." (Need any more be said?) But he insisted on questioning me further about being born again. He didn't understand that being a member of a church was good enough to make me a Christian. We parted company because I wasn't "saved."

Mom suggested we go to the priest at Advance, because if Becky were of our faith, she would be in that parish. Recognizing this as potentially our last shot, before we went in I pulled Becky aside for a talk. "Becky," I said, "If you agree to raise the kids in my church, I won't hold you to it."

"Okay," she replied. "Then, we just won't have any kids." So, we went before that priest (a holy man of God) and lied through our teeth. We were married on November 15, 1969. Becky's aunts all showed up, but not one uncle. It was opening day of deer season.

I don't know about the uncles, but that year I got my dear.

CHAPTER 14
TREACHEROUS TENTACLES

Satan is presented in Scripture as being subtle and complex. "We wrestle not against flesh and blood." The nature of the fight is one of internally wrestling many tentacles, like the seizing grips of an octopus. Vietnam was only one of these tentacles. It's amazing how insidious Satan's tentacles can be. In spite of everything good I now had with Becky, hatred for Oscar continued coiled around my soul. Its entangling tentacle had wrapped me so tightly and burrowed so far down to the bone that nothing could break its grip.

It is written of bitterness: "Beware, lest a root of bitterness rise up and defile many."

When you drop rocks into a pond, perfect concentric circles form on the surface. A person's life, dropped into this world, generates a rhythm of waves that lap all surrounding waters, causing minute increments of help or harm. My life had become a rock of bitterness, robbed of joyful interaction, rippling its bitterness out to contaminate others.

Satan wanted to continue using my pattern of relationships to defile everyone who would come into my life. So, it was in his best interest to do everything he could to delay my emancipation as long as possible. Even after I was to become free of his stranglehold, he would come back often to refresh the habits of bitterness again and again.

The tentacle of parental rejection also held me in bondage.Real or imagined, I never felt I was good enough for my parents.

My dad always seemed to have a different definition of success than I could either fully define or grasp. Therefore, success was always an uncertain territory. By contrast, failure was a very certain and well explored territory. I now see that failure actually began to feel comfortable. One learns to desire what is familiar, and default to it.

I didn't measure up, and felt parental disappointment, but this was familiar pain; I could cope with it. Good grades and achievement, on the other hand, were unknown territory. I didn't know what such change might bring-what fresh new forms of torture and ridicule, confusion and demand. So, I chose to remain where I felt comfortable. It is a shame, in a way, that giving up on meeting my parent's expectations and approval never led to open rebellion. If it had, perhaps I would have stood a chance of blowing open the lockbox I was shut up in. Instead, deciding it was impossible to work hard enough to please my parents, I agonized at working hard not to displease them.

This anxiety slapped another bumper sticker label on my life: Sissy. Anyone who worried about displeasing parents was a sissy. Under all the mocking bumper stickers, my life was a vehicle of hopelessness. Even though I was convinced it didn't pay to serve God, becoming an altar boy was part of the process of appeasing my parents. I became a master at masking the misery of who I was on the inside with a shell of obedient posture on the outside. Psychologists call these two identities the person and the personage. The person is who you are on the inside, and the personage is who you let others see. The closer the two, the better the state of mental health a person enjoys. The further apart, the greater a persons' mental pain.

In early years, you explore what happens when you expose your person to other people's personages.

In that process, if rejection is received and internalized, you learn to hide your exposed person under an artificial personage. They remain two separate and irreconcilable identities. If in the process acceptance is received and internalized, you learn to fold your person and personage into a richly creative blend of independent authenticity.

Because there was no continuity between who I was inside and out, I was completely lacking in confidence. I was a lie waiting to be discovered. As a result, the fate of my life was always held in the hands of another-whoever happened to be the most present, the most powerful, the most feared, or the most envied.

Back in the jungles, I had come to believe if I could just beatVietnam, all would be well with my life and with the world. I would become a hero on the inside and the outside. And the Great War for my soul would be over. I had gone to Vietnam to jettison all the misery of my life into a foreign county, and leave it there. Pity it didn't work that way. This was a battle that had to be won on home soil.

About a week after Becky and I married, she began playing Ethel Water's album, His Eye is on the Sparrow; I know He's Watching Me. This was not my kind of music. Ethel Waters had no business reminding me of the Lord. And I didn't want Him Watching Me when I wasn't looking. So, when Becky was out shopping, I hid the record under the sofa, and the tug of war fell my way.I didn't begrudge God his place in my church. I even had respectable measure of appreciation for Him there. I wanted Him to be someplace where I could stop by from time to time to visit. But I wanted Him to stay in His assigned place. I needed a form of religion to protect me from the inner darkness and squeezing grips that frightened me-like a cross held out to ward off a vampire. I wanted a good luck icon god. Something I could rub from time to time for comfort.

But I didn't want a god who would demand I let loose of my precious grievances-my comfortable monotony-my bitterness and hatred. Wait a minute! Was this a discovery? Could it be possible I was not being held against my will by an enemy's grip? Could it be that the tentacles of bitterness and rejection that bound me had grown up in the garden of my own soul? That it wasn't Oscar's long arm of destruction, but my own, that threatened to strangle me. The stones of bitterness and rejection were in my clutch; I wasn't in theirs. And I curled them into the core of my being like dark, ferreted treasure.

CHAPTER 15
SOULLESS IN TENNESSEE

After we got married, Becky and I grubbed by on a $100 a week paycheck from F.W. Woolworth Co., Main Street, Cape Girardeau. My first job there, Assistant Manager, was a lofty title for stock boy. I had to wear a suit, white shirt, and a tie, but they put me to work unloading freight. The worst part of this job was my ego. In the Marine Corps, I was a sergeant, and that was next to God. Here, I was a young man, scraping humbly for any break. But marriage was a sweet balm over injured ego and struggles of the soul. I turned my full attention to marital bliss and career aspirations, and after just a few months in Cape Girardeau, I was transferred to Nashville. What a great place to go! We were quickly moving up the corporate ladder to heaven. If I had any doubts about my awesome potential, they vanished when the store manager took his vacation right after we arrived, and left me in charge. What an ego trip!

But after we were in Nashville about a year, my old torments began to haunt me again. Every night before bed, Becky always read her Bible, and invariably, from the text she read, she would ask me what something meant. I'd read it with her and make up an answer. I had all the answers. If she didn't know the difference, that made me right by default and swelled my ego. But, in truth, these brief exposures to scripture, as limited as they were, were creating in me a great contention. On the underside of my soul, Satan was eating me up with guilt and bitterness, while on the upper side of my soul God was peeling back layers of empty religious repetition.

Becky, with her gentle persistence and unconditional love, was providing a safe place for God's probing.

In pursuit of relief from the war raging within me, I went to see a priest and asked him how I could be delivered from the anguish of uncertainty.

"How can I know if have eternal life?"

He said, "If I knew that, I'd help myself."

"Great! A priest is supposed to know these things. Why do I go to him if he doesn't have answers?"

It was clear I would have to find the answers I needed outside of my church. But every new place I turned for clarity gave me a different answer. A tumble of mixed signals crowded in until my soul was in total confusion. The Old Testament tells of those who express the pain of grief and anguish by tearing their clothing. I felt like I needed to rend my mind and life in two, and let the confusion and pain gush out in relief. I felt I could no longer bear the pressure of my bulging mental pain. I contemplated suicide again. I had believed a tour in the Marine Corps would resolve the pain of my youth, but it had just carved the pain into greater relief.

I had thought the brutal shock of a Vietnam War would clear the avalanching weight of failed expectations, but it had only come near to collapsing the weight with its own failures. Suicide might relieve my conflict, but, then again, if there was a hell waiting, I might be jumping from a bonfire of pain into a roaring forest fire, without hope of end. The Marines and Vietnam had failed me. So, why should death bring me an expected resolution?

Besides, I didn't want to die. I wanted to scream for help. So, I overdosed and was taken to the hospital. They just pumped my stomach and sent me home.

"Doesn't it mean anything to anybody that I tried to kill myself?" I had cried out in desperation, but no one knew what to do except send me home. "Emptiness, emptiness, all is emptiness."

My parents didn't have the answer, the Marines didn't have the answer, a bloody war didn't have the answer, and the clergy didn't have the answer, the hospital didn't have the answer, and work didn't have the answer. What did that leave?

The shame of it all was that I had a wife who loved me in spite of myself, and I didn't know how to love her back. Bitterness had killed my ability to love. My inner man was so far removed from my outer man that they were nothing more than two halves of a shell, hiding a pit of emptiness. I was lost; Satan had won. "What will a man give in exchange for his soul?"

I wasn't sure what I had exchanged for mine, or just when, exactly, I had packaged it up and shipped it off, but I was sure of one thing. It was gone. Esau sold his soul for a bowl of beans. I had sold my soul and apparently gotten nothing in exchange.

What can a man do without a soul?

CHAPTER 16
FREE AT LAST

After the suicide attempt, Woolworth's fired me. But Stanley Home Products was willing to give me a chance to kill myself at door-to-door sales. I got six traffic tickets in the next three months. I was certain to lose my license. On the last ticket, Billie Vaughn, a friend drove me to court. The judge said, "Well, Mr. Hutchings, since this is your first offense . . ." (This was before computers).

To avoid tickets, I changed my job to work at Furniture World. Each morning I had to cross the Old Hickory Bridge and the speed limit changed from 40 MPH to 25 MPH. Of course, I got more tickets.

One morning a policeman in civilian clothes came shopping. He saw me and approached asking if I was George Hutchings and did I drive a yellow Vega. "Yes, that is me." He said the police had a pool going on me crossing the bridge.

When the police know you by name and car, it is time to leave town. We figured it was only a matter of time before the Nashville Police Department realized their mistake. Becky and I moved back to St. Louis, hoping there was no extradition treaty.

Prior to the move, Levitz Furniture Store had promised me a job in St. Louis, but by the time I arrived, management had changed and "No job" seemed the name of that tune. Wicks Furniture did hire me, though, and once again, it seemed the pendulum was swinging our way.

My home town is only about 150 miles from St. Louis; so many weekends were spent on the Interstate headed home.

We may have intended those weekends to be R&R, but under the façade they were something far different for me. The highway led to my home town and to my unresolved bitterness and anger. When you ache in your bones, you can't stand to stay still. In the same way, the bones of my bitterness and anger ached for rest so intensely I had to stir them from time to time for some measure of relief.

No amount of reasoning, wrestling, or disillusionment had dissuaded me from believing that all the bad in my life could be atoned for in the death of Oscar. If anything, the relentless stream of failures since leaving home had burgeoned the conviction. And these frequent trips back home had stirred the embers of ache into open flame once again. Fantasies about a day of atonement started to take on a life of their own.

Oscar didn't live at home any longer. Married now, he had built a house behind his parent's. I knew he used bottled gas at his home, a convenient cover up for an explosion. But Central Hardware didn't carry bombs, so the only explosive available was gasoline. "Too complicated and sloppy."

The beauty of simplicity was far more alluring. So, I took my new .22 rifle and explored the hill facing his house. I couldn't find a single vantage point with a clean shot, and I reasoned someone would see my car leaving. While caught up in my debate, Oscar stepped out on the porch. Cross hairs split his temple. "Now! Do it now," I commanded myself.

Suddenly I was repeating the suspended moments before the trigger had jumped in Vietnam. These were the last remaining seconds of opportunity for change. Once again I was at this place. The defeat of utter emptiness swept through me. And Oscar moved off the porch, out of my sights yet again.

GEORGE P. HUTCHINGS - COMBAT SURVIVAL

After that, every night I'd wake up scared stiff. The hair on the back of my neck would stand on end, and it felt like an evil presence had me in the grip of paralysis. The only defense I had against the monster was to take something to help me sleep. In the morning everything would appear to be okay once again.

One day, Al Guarney and his wife bought some furniture from me. They were nice people, and after the purchase, they did something no one had ever done in my life. They invited me to church.

"I can't do that. I already have a church," I said. "Oh, we have the best preacher west of the Mississippi River," they boasted. I had always wanted to hear a good preacher. The ones I had heard didn't have anything to say. When the Guarneys gave me the name of the church and the time of services, I accepted the information. That night I told Becky we were going to attend on Sunday, and she said, "No. The church right down the street made a visit and left a pamphlet on the door. We need to go there."

"No we aren't," I heard myself say. "That guy can't preach a lick. And I want to hear a good preacher." The Guarneys had become my authorities on who was and wasn't the best preacher in town. Becky said okay.

By Friday night of that week, I was unraveling on all seams, spilling out an engorgement of hurt, bitterness, and anger. I couldn't carry the infestation any further. I went to confession, but all I could do was weep. The priest pitied me. "Go on home and dry your tears," he said. "Everything will be okay."

I went out to the car and wept so inconsolably Becky thought I was going nuts. But I pulled my seams together and made it to Sunday. That morning we drove halfway across the city to judge for ourselves if the Guarneys had anything worth bragging about.

I had always heard how Christians loved and cared for one another. Was this true? Did the church know anything about Semper Fi? I figured Al Guarney wouldn't even be at the church that morning, but there he was, expecting me.

As part of church procedure, we were given a visitor's card which included the question, "Do you want a pastoral visit, yes or no?" If everything I'd ever done in my life up to this point wasn't going to send me to hell, this surely would, because here I was in a Baptist Church. According to my indoctrination, if I invited the preacher of another faith into my home, I would be guilty of a mortal sin. But I wanted this preacher to visit me, so while I swiped a hand across my eyes, I checked as close to the "yes" spot as I could, like pinning the tail on the donkey, and threw it in the offering plate. It was a random accident. Any sin can be justified if it's an accident.

Fear over my reckless "yes" kept me from hearing anything else that entire church service, but afterwards something remarkable happened. Grover and Betty Kimble, two people we didn't even know, invited us to their home for dinner. We reflected on the peanut butter and crackers waiting for us at our house, and decided this was a much better offer. Their hospitality was incredible. No booze, no smoking, no foul language, but the most fun we had known in along, long time. "Where were we, Mars? The comfort of love pervaded their home and created a safe place for hostile emotions to loosen.

Christian people knew something about, Semper Fi, and I approved.

The following evening, we had a knock on our door. It was the Sunday preacher. He was 6'4", and the peephole only came up to his chin. Apparently my "donkey's tail" had come close enough to the "yes" to win a prize. I turned the light off and sat down in the dark, whispering,

"The preacher is here."

"Didn't you invite him?" Becky replied.

I was caught, "Just a minute, preacher." I put my necktie on. If I was going to meet the preacher, I had to measure up. Apparently I had a lot of confidence in the powers of a polyester tie. After an extended and patient wait on our porch step, I finally opened the door and invited Rev. Robert S. Whitehead to come in.

I offered him a beer. He politely declined. I offered him a cigar. He politely declined. Then it was his turn to ask a question. "George, if you were to die tonight, do you know for certain you would go to heaven?," and it was my turn to answer.

"No preacher."

He said, "Then get me your Bible." This was important because my Bible differed from his Bible. His Bible could have been marked like a deck of cards, but he was willing to play with my deck. I relaxed. This preacher was unarmed. He didn't string me along in suspense, either. He took me straight to the core of my anguished desire: Turning my Bible to 1 John 5:13 he read as I looked at the script. "These things have I written, that you might know that you have eternal life, and that you might believe on the name of the Son of God." Rev. Whitehead said, "George, the whole Bible was written so that you can know that you can have eternal life."

I said, "All my life I've been told this knowledge isn't possible."

He then proceeded to show me the passage: "The wages of sin is death." The paycheck for sin was death. What was difficult to understand about a paycheck analogy? Nothing, it was very clear. He asked, "The sin mentioned here, is it a mortal sin or a venial sin?" "Well," I replied, "it just says sin."

"So, regardless of whatever kind of sin, if you were to die tonight with even one sin on your soul, where would you spend eternity?" My reply came without hesitation. I'd known the answer to that one for a long time. "Hell."

He showed me the passage: "While you were yet sinners, Christ died for you." Christ died in my place? He paid the price for my sin? I remembered Corporal Bice.

But what did I have to do to claim this incomprehensible absolution? He then showed me: "Whosoever will call on the name of the Lord shall be saved." All I had to do was call, and He would answer? I told the preacher of my anguish after seeing the priest, and the broken cry of my heart for forgiveness. He said I may have already cried out for the mercy and grace of new birth, even though I hadn't understood.

"Would you like to pray again now, with faith and understanding?" he asked. "It might free of you doubt." Yes, I did want this-with all my heart, with all my past, my present, and my future. As we bowed to pray, a deep spiritual surgery took place. The tentacles of Satan were cut loose from their stranglehold on my heart, soul, and mind. And I let go of the darkness I had guarded and savored, all of my conscious life. Just as the curtain that separated God and man was rent in two at the time of the Cross, the conflicts of my life were rent in two right there.

The facade of my bitter outer man fell away like a massive ugly cocoon, and the naked wounds of my soul spilled out its bitterness and hatred in streams of sorrow.

The flowing presence of the Lord and His provision swept clean the canyons of my life. And the refreshment was profound.

Tears of cleansing and relief racked me as layer after layer of my sin was exposed, confessed, repented, and abandoned like litter, to be carried away on the waters that flowed through me with cleansing.

The entanglements of Satan were being cut loose. Just as "God breathed into Adam, and man became a living soul," He also breathed into the barren, waterless dust of my life. And George became a living soul.

In that single breath, my present and future were given life and reason, and my past was given reason, too. I could now see that every experience I had ever gone through had been ordained to lead me to this moment of truth, when I would find eternal life.

God knew I didn't consider myself a sinner, and He was fully aware of the incredible resistance I had to that truth, so He had, given me the experience of a little boy strike into my heart and would be known as sin. The first act I considered sin was my true condition.

Knowing my every point of spiritual need, His "hounds" had herded me with deliberate persistence toward the gates of His love. The Lord had allowed me to peek into Hell on October 12, 1967 and acknowledged hell as my eternal domicile. I was reminded of the words given me by the doctor, long ago in Japan, "Remember the hounds of heaven." Then there was Bice dying in my place. Later, I would believe to be killed on March 15th but was wounded on the 18th the three days of the resurrection.

Being a fisherman, another analogy also came to mind. A good fisherman knows how to keep a tight line while slowly allowing the fish to exhaust his strength. Jesus, the fisher of men, had mastered my catch. He had drawn me out of the polluted cesspool of my own waste and now He was setting me free in the living waters of a new life.

That new life meant activity, purpose and mission. I couldn't wait to get started!

Right then and there, I knew God had called me to preach and I promised to follow him to anyplace but Africa.

First order of business was to set Oscar free. Hatred had been purged from my life and I was anxious to let Oscar know. I didn't delay in driving to my home town to present the white flag of peace, assuming full responsibility for the years of bitterness and struggle. What a tragedy my entire youth, had been ravaged with such disease.

All those years, when I could have been exploring and loving life, I had clutched this death to my chest instead. Now, by the grace of God, it fell away from me like the weight of a mountain, and I could finally see the glorious landscape that stretched before me. My hope was that Oscar and I might actually become friends, but when nothing jelled, I let it go. No more negative obsessions for me, but there became an obsession that was fun. The fellowship with other believers such as Harold and Mary O'Dell brought love and laughter. My father introduced me to whoppers and Harold became an unwitting candidate.

Harold and Mary O'Dell lived one block from us and attended the same church. They often invited Becky and me for after church dinner. We became such friends that in spite of their parental age that I often stopped in for coffee on the way to work. Harold was a farm boy transplanted to the city by Monsanto. The telling of tall stories became a manor of life but I won the contest.

Becky and I had a large back yard and I needed a tiller to plant a garden. Harold had a man eater tiller and laughed when I asked to borrow it.

He told me that the people who borrowed it never came home but the tiller always made it back. What does that mean? I don't know but we put it in his truck and delivered the man eater to my house.

The tiller would start but I could not control it. That blasted machine ran ahead of me and made a hole in the fence quite visible to our neighbor. After several days of trying to plow my garden, I gave up. The tiller wins, but Harold can never know that this farm boy could not use a tiller.

I had one more friend and we delivered the tiller back to Harold. I bragged about how good the garden looked and that I had planted a lot of tomatoes. Harold drove by my house on his way to work everyday. He tried to spot the garden but I kept the gate closed and the garden (or lack thereof) hidden away. All summer long, I bragged about the tomatoes to the point of buying some farm fresh tomatoes and delivering them to him. He was fatherly proud of son George the farmer.

In the autumn of the year Harold came to my house but I was not home. He wanted to see the garden and walked to the back of the house. The only thing he saw was rabbits. The next time he saw me he asked if the rabbits had eaten my garden! He was a good sport and I believe we are friends to this day. Every time he sees me he asks about my mator (Southeast Missouri Accent) patch. Yeah, life is good.

Dr. Sutherland and George working out the English problems.

CHAPTER 17
ENGLISH 113 & EDUCATION 101

Pastor Whitehead introduced me to baptism. It went something like this: George when you were a Marine you wore the uniform of a Marine. That uniform identified you as being a Marine. The Lord has called you to be a soldier in His army and his uniform is baptism. I asked, "Does the Lord have a Marine Corps, don't think much about the Army?" The pastor said, "I'll dunk you twice." The concept was clear so there were no problems. Becky was afraid to join the church or get baptized. Still gripped by her previous church teaching, she was sure lightening would strike her. But after I was baptized and not killed, she joined up.

The first thing our pastor emphasized to help us learn our way through this newly discovered adventure, was reading the Bible. Reading the Bible? Where do I start? In spite of all my religious up bringing, I didn't know the Old Testament from the New Testament. I called PSALMS - "Palms," JOB - "job" and thought John 3:16 was the men's room on the third floor, suite 16. All religious participation prior to this revolution in my soul had been nothing more than inattentive motion. Now, I was engaged! I began reading scripture, and my soul soaked it up like fresh spring water.

As scripture were read, more questions came. Answers to one question brought more and more questions. For the first time, I could feel God himself talking with my soul. My soul was being fed spiritual food, and I was becoming a whole person.

One big cavern that had to be backfilled was legalism. The mini-skirt was in vogue, but I wouldn't let Becky wear a dress that didn't reach to the floor.

GEORGE P. HUTCHINGS - COMBAT SURVIVAL

We couldn't go to movies and couldn't listen to rock music. We had to go to church for Sunday School and worship service. We had to be back that night for Church Training and worship. Tuesday night was visitation, and Wednesday night was prayer meeting.

None of this was forced; we were just so hungry for spiritual food we didn't want to miss any opportunities. This hyper activity it did feed a spiritual ego. After all, only the faithful made all the services; everyone else wasn't dedicated. This was legalism mixed with superstition. If I lived my life just right, everything would be fine. If I read my Bible, attended church, and prayed three times each day, then God would be good to us. I got so clean I squeaked when I walked. Something was wrong, however. It wasn't fun any more. People started avoiding me, and I didn't even like my own company. I had a lot of growing in grace to do.

All new Christians learn that "New Birth" is not the finish line . . . it was the opening line of a whole new adventure. "New birth" was followed by "new living", and this new spiritual living had as many twists and turns as its physical counterpart. Detours, perplexities, and challenges were as present in this "new life" as the joyous discoveries of hope and possibility were. But the uncommon denominator between this "new life" and my "old life" was that this route was actually leading, without fail, someplace I wanted to go, Heaven. And pilgrims on this journey were commissioned to travel light, free of guilt, bitterness, and the curse of uncertainty.

Though the promise of heaven was already given to me, its physical reality awaited me at the end of the journey. The providence of God was going to lead me in exploring the best forks in the road to take me there. Every one of the forks led "home" (and it would be impossible to ever completely lose my way), yet there was one scenic route plotted out specifically for my life. The great pleasure of this new life was discovering what next He had placed before me.

GEORGE P. HUTCHINGS - COMBAT SURVIVAL

One of the first bends in the road would take me home. Since the change of direction in our lives, we had stayed away from family. We had not begun to serve in a different church to deliberately hurt them, but we knew it would, and we didn't want to press the issue. Then one day we got a call that Dad was in the hospital with another of his annual heart attacks. Uncertain of his spiritual peace, and concerned he might die without understanding, I set out on the drive to see him. I knew it was time to explain my new faith.

We owned two Bibles, a Douay Version and a King James Version. I figured if I couldn't find what I needed to say in one, I could find it in the other. So I had brought them both. Mom met me in the parking lot, saw the Bibles, and in tears asked, "What have you done? Gone off and got yourself mixed up with some strange religion?"

I told her I had experienced salvation and wanted to tell Dad before he died. She didn't want me to see him. But I knew if I was right and she was wrong, we had everything to lose. But if I was wrong, she stood to lose nothing. I found the courage to walk past her defiance and into my dad's room. He was sleeping, but woke right up. I can't recall the exact conversation, but I will never forget his bitter disappointment and disapproval. He later wrote, calling me a son of the devil, and said I had "defected to the enemy."

Men act according to conviction; boys are afraid to grasp the truth and take a position. I was finally learning to reach for what counted whatever the cost. In this case, it cost me my family, but, "What will a man give in exchange for his soul?" Esau sold his soul for a plate of beans. What would I give in exchange for my soul, my family? The changes I had made were not simply emotional fads. They had been embraced in both body and mind, with rational mental assent. This new faith was the difference between heaven and hell. Pain could now be endured because I had a purpose.

Out of a heart of love I had gone to see my dad, knowing he would reject me. In spite of the pain, I did it because it was right.

This "New Birth" was beginning to make a man out of an overgrown boy. Paul describes the Christian life as that of a soldier. He has to gather the courage to go to battle and the strength to finish the fight. I looked pretty awful during those first days of fighting the Christian battle. The excitement of the new birth was greater than watching Rocky II and the newness of the experience demanded its telling. I wanted to share it. But I was just a new pilgrim, growing in grace and knowledge, understanding little of the Bible. What I didn't know, I made up for in overbearing persistence.

One night, Becky was watching a vampire movie, Count Yorga. Dad would never let us watch horror movies, so I had never seen a vampire movie before in my life. The movie was good, and I got caught up in it. Becky, who had seen it a hundred times, got bored, and went to bed.

In the movie's last scene, the hero is fighting off vampires with a cross. He backs them down into a cellar and locks the door. The last image is of him turning to give his girlfriend a hug and a kiss on the back of her neck. What he doesn't know is that the vampires have gotten her. Now she is giving him a hug and a bite on the back of his neck.

"Oh no!" I cried. Becky jumped out of bed, thinking I had suffered a heart attack.

"I'm okay. I just thought the vampires got me." The show was over, so it was time for lights out. The moon was shining through the window, casting a spooky aura over the bed. Becky turned her head to kiss me good night and light reflected off her teeth. No way, not me! I was on the sofa the rest of the night, pouring through the book of concordance.

GEORGE P. HUTCHINGS - COMBAT SURVIVAL

Life brought a lot of questions for which I didn't have answers. Was there such a spiritual force as vampires? (I knew one thing for sure. There would never be another vampire in my house if I had anything to say about it!)

Here I was, convinced God was calling me to preach, and I didn't even know reality from vampires. How do you respond to the dilemma of a new direction and too little preparedness? I decided it would be good to study. Twice I impulsively enrolled in college and twice I impulsively quit. But once again, I enrolled. This time I stuck it out, in spite of the old trials that were to rear their tentacles again.

I had been told by others that my calling was probably to be an evangelist. An evangelist preached at our church, and after hearing him I understood why. A pastor stays with one church, nurturing one group toward growth and maturity. An evangelist travels to different churches, stirring up trouble and then leaving. Since I didn't think I had the depth of character or knowledge to pastor a church, then, by default, I was surely called to evangelism.

While in college, I struck up a quick friendship with two pastors. One of them asked me to preach a revival at his church. The meeting went great. I had one sermon, but preached it three times. The people were happy and the pastor was happy-or so I thought-and I went home. On Monday, however, there was a different spirit in the air when I saw my friend back at the college.

Methodically, he picked my sermon apart. Then, in the cafeteria he ignored my invitation to sit. The next day I got my coffee and started to join him, but he said my name rather loudly, and then dropped his voice and began to mumble to his tablemate. This was an old Oscar tactic. His attitude had clearly changed to scorn, and he felt it was his obligation, apparently, to deprive me of any notion that I was worthy of his company or respect.

The tension continued to escalate until one class session he deliberately mocked every answer I attempted to offer in class, completely humiliating me before everyone else. Suddenly, Christ's words, "Overcome evil with good," were swept away by remembrance of God telling Joshua to completely destroy the Philistines. Inside my body there still lived a proud Marine, and I voted for Joshua.

Cutting my opponent off at the door, I put my right index finger solidly upon his chest. Backing him across the room with one jab of the finger after another, he was told, "I don't take rejection very well. If you ever challenge another one of my answers; I will pick up a chair and beat you about your head and shoulders. In class, during class, out of class-cross me and your butt is mine." Then I turned to his accomplice and said, "That goes for you, too. One at a time, or all at once, it's on!"

They never gave me any more problems, but I had lost a major war. Satan had gotten me by the stranglehold again-rejection and humiliation, rage and bitterness. My high school fears flooded back in; I was crazy, and no "New Birth" could change that. One day, I had bloody hands, the next day clean hands. One day I was approved, the next day disapproved, grades were bad, and peer pressure remained. It all tangled together in a crazy mix. But in the midst of Satan's attack, I found a strand of scripture to carry me:

"God has not given us the Spirit of fear, but of love and of power, and of a sound mind." Everyday I was to see my failures and rejection, but in spite of the evidence, I believed God for a sound mind.

College had been a whole new start, but it was obvious my attitude carried a lot of old baggage. Besides rejection and fear, I still carried arrogance and pride. My first professor was Dr. William Muncie.

He was the author of several textbooks, had been the pastor of numerous churches, and had been a professor for over twenty years. This man was well-known, well-loved, and well-respected, but not by me. I took one look at him and said to myself, "I wonder if he is saved."

My whole life I had been led around by others, taking their word for things. No more! After class, I went up to my professor and asked brazenly, "Dr. Muncy, are you saved? I don't want to learn anything about religion from anybody who isn't saved." Dr. Muncy was well-loved for a reason. He answered my impudent question in the kindest manner. His grace extracted the pain of fear and freed me for an increment of growth-and hope.

Perhaps someday, I would reflect Dr. Muncy's kindness. Dr. Sutherland wasn't so mild. He had been a military man, and had retired as a high-ranking officer. His official class was English 113, but Dr. Sutherland taught another unlisted course- perseverance. I was just back from Vietnam and all I knew was to cuss and fire and M-16. Dr. Sutherland had no use for either. Less than one year ago, I was a sergeant giving orders and taking names. I had respect. Now I was a college freshman where no one gets respect. His English 113 course was such an enjoyable, I took it over three times. He corrected my deficits with barbed wit, and smiled disarmingly as he failed me from the course all three semesters.

I later took the course under another professor and passed, but I took as many writing courses as possible with Dr. Sutherland. He wouldn't let me get by without my best. It came to be that I wanted to do well, but also that I didn't want to let him down. I could suffer humiliation if there was a purpose and a chance for redemption. I was getting an education in more ways than one.

Dr. Sutherland and the Russian girls.

CHAPTER 18
BIG FREEZE, BIG DOGS, & BIG PROFESSOR

Hertz Rental Company needed a truck delivered to Ft. Worth, Texas and we happened to be going that way. I drove the truck, and Becky drove our van. We were barely out of Missouri when the rental truck's clutch went out. A call back to St. Louis informed us that the clutch had just been replaced. Unfortunately, bolts for a car, not for a two-ton truck, had been used. Thanks to one mechanic who thought bolt size was optional, we were left stranded on the highway for two days in January!

The situation was about to get much worse. It was 1978 the year of the big freeze. Everybody knows Texas is a hot state. It seldom, if ever, snows there. But we crossed the Arkansas border into snow-logged traffic that was backed all the up to Ft. Worth, over 300 miles away. One is tempted to exaggerate stories, but there isn't any wiggle room for exaggeration in this story. It busts its own seams with disbelief. We were stopped so long in that marathon traffic jam snow and ice completely covered the car. It was our first experience with camping in a freeway igloo.

When we finally arrived at Southwestern Seminary, we were more than ready to burrow into our warm new home. Except we didn't know where it was, and Southwestern Seminary was closed due to snow. This was the first time the seminary had ever closed. Fortunately, Mike Anthony, a friend from college, noticed us in traffic, ran us down, and led us to the house.

What a sight that new home was after our grueling dog-sled trek from Missouri!

GEORGE P. HUTCHINGS - COMBAT SURVIVAL

Things would be smooth sailing from here on. Confidently, we backed the truck up to the garage to unload, only to discover that the metal truck door and power lift were frozen shut. We hammered, picked, and probably swore, but the door wouldn't budge. Mike went out and bought a flamethrower, stood back about 15 feet, and let it roar. The whole world started sweating!

"Mike!" I hollered. "The gas tank is right under the door!" Fortunately, he managed to break the door loose without the gas tank exploding.

From our first experience crossing the Arkansas line, Texas was a real trip. It was, for two country bumpkins from Southeast Missouri, what missionaries call culture shock. We had a new climate, no family, a hectic pace of academic work, new jobs, new friends, and new church.

Becky wrote her mother, putting her return address as "Ft. Worthless." She was always reflecting on how to more accurately express her feelings about the big state of Texas. Sometimes her reflections were subtle. "If I owned hell and if I owned Texas, I'd live in hell and rent out Texas." (And sometimes they weren't so subtle.)

Texas was a land of contrasts. After that extreme winter, the summer heat was blistering enough to melt our toothbrushes. I remember looking out the window one morning to see why traffic was honking. There was my wife, in the middle of the road, the bottom of her plastic shoes melted, binding her to the oozing asphalt. I had to ford the asphalt goop, pick her up (hearing her shoes release with a sucking blurb), sling her over my shoulder, and carry her to safety.

If you don't believe that, then try this one. I once called home and asked the operator to keep the time and charges. After the call, she said, "That will be $38." I said, "Ma'am, I could have called hell and back for that." She said, "Sir that would have been a local call."

GEORGE P. HUTCHINGS - COMBAT SURVIVAL

As if the summer wasn't enough to kill us, in 1979 the six o'clock news carried the story of a gas line leak. Gas had gone through the sewer and was coming up through the bathtub drains. One man filled his lungs while it while taking a shower. (I don't think he meant to strike oil that morning.) When he flipped the light switch off, he became a living bomb. There's no need to embellish stories in Texas. Reality is big enough.

Dealing with Texas' bigger than life ego wasn't the only thing we were grappling with while in seminary. It seemed that everything had to be thought out again, including our prenuptial agreement.

Becky still didn't want children. But the idyllic notion of children had begun to grow on me with a passion. Even I knew having kids was about more than idyllic notion, though. Everybody knows raising kids responsibly requires a certain depth of character. Since my "depth of character" had, from time to time, come into question, I pondered this concern. How could I find out if I'd make a good dad?

Dogs! That was the ticket! If I could take care of dogs, the same would obviously be true of children. A good friend had two pointers up for adoption, and a man couldn't ask for a better dog to prove his mettle. Pointers are great bird dogs. They're big. And they can run and play. They are dogs a man can be proud to own. So we got the two dogs.One died and the other ran away. I never mentioned kids again.

My depth of character had other areas to explore. One was learning to appreciate and submit to the professors who were predestined (and some might say cursed) with the task of trying to take a vampire-ignorant country boy and shape him up for the ministry. (I still had cowlicks of impudence and ignorance, too, even after college.) Perhaps Dr. David Fite, the professor of pastoral ministries, was the most remarkable of these elect.

Dr. Fite sat behind his desk in a three-piece suit enjoying a cushy job, as far as I could see. The heels of his shoes weren't even worn. What right did he have to teach me about the hardships of the ministry? What qualified him to carry the title, Professor of Pastoral Ministries? He didn't know anything about having to give up family for the ministry. Pastors had never cheated him or his wife and openly mocked his preaching. Here was a man who didn't even know what pain was, telling me about "pastoral ministry." More than once the words, "You can't help if you haven't felt," were on the tip of my tongue in his class. To complete my disdain, Dr. Fite's class seemed to center almost exclusively on the ministry of pastor. I was an evangelist.

What was I, dog meat? One day the plight of poorly paid preachers came up, and was being belabored and bemoaned by the entire class. One sad Sam story after another was told about being underappreciated and underpaid in the work of pastor. Each story tried to top the previous in pity score.

Having stood all the "pastor whining" I could stomach, I rose to my feet and said, "You fellas work in one church, with a following of consistent members, knowing exactly where you're going to be the next Sunday and the next, and exactly what your paycheck is going to be to meet the bills. An evangelist has to find 52 places of work each year, never knowing where or if another call will come. The evangelist is forced to leave family and loved ones for much of the year, and never knows for sure whether or not there will be money to pay the bills. I'm tired of coming here to hear all about the problems of poor pastors." The bell rang and class dismissed without another word. I had strutted my stuff, and it felt good. Dr. Fite should thank me for teaching him a thing or two.

In the third month of class, I learned a little more about Dr. Fite. It turned out; he had been a missionary in Cuba when Castro took over. He was thrown in jail and didn't see his newborn baby for six years.

GEORGE P. HUTCHINGS - COMBAT SURVIVAL

The only food he got for those entire six years was one cup of rice a day, unless you count the maggots that crawled through it. His wife, a respected schoolteacher, was reduced to custodial work and public disgrace. Prison officials taunted Dr. Fite with graphic details about how his wife had been seen cheating on him.

Not being allowed a Bible, Dr. Fite somehow got hold of some chalk and began writing the scriptures in Greek. Other inmates asked him explain what he was writing and Dr. Fite became known as the prison chaplain. He won countless numbers to the faith. I felt lower than a snake's belly in a wagon rut, but I was about to feel even lower. Not only was Dr. Fite a giant of a man in ministry, he was also a man of practical humility and grace.

Texas summers are hot, but when it rains, it pours. The ground is so hard the water runs off it like cement. Our back yard sloped towards the house so the water came over like a spillway, through the brick, and into the bedroom and hallway, drenching our carpeting.

We lived in the same subdivision as Dr. Fite, but I didn't even know he was aware of this until he appeared at our front door in bib overalls to help pull up the carpet. In his quiet, capable manner, he showed me how to keep the carpeting up off the floor so it could dry. Hardly a word was said, but I had heard volumes. I gazed upon his beauty. And felt the shame of my twisted pride. Beauty has extraordinary power. It picks people up. Ugliness is depressing. Beauty heals the ugliness of life. Dr. Fite was a beautiful sight, reminding me of the testimony of another, "We beheld His glory."

Thanks to the presence of such beauty, we survived the big freeze, the big dog discouragement, the big professor lessons, and the big blindness of my pride. Texas and its seminary was over.

It was now time to take that healing to others. Our first church position lay just ahead.

CHAPTER 19
LOVE OFFERING LEVY

It was 1980, and we were still in Ft. Worth, Texas, entertaining some family, Charles and Marian. They had made the trip from Missouri on a motorcycle as a mini-vacation from their demanding photography business. The evening was refreshing. School was completed. My job was forgotten. And our family had come out of their way to see us. Since the break in family relations over our church differences, Becky and I were both anxious to re-establish a bonding family unit.

Charles and Marian's trip was a turning point. It was good to feel natural affection again. When the phone interrupted our visit, it was the pastor of a church in St. Louis. He wanted me to come on staff as the Minister of Education. We had known each other a long time, so we were under no disillusionments; we had definite differences. Could we work past those differences well enough to serve a church together?

The pleasant evening was suddenly fraught with the pressure of uncertainty.Rather than draw a regular salary, my friend had convinced his church to pay the pastor by "love offering". The agreement was that the promotion of the love offering would never be brought to the church's attention. The Pastor called it living in secret with God.

I told my friend my view on his "love offering" arrangement for ministry personnel had not changed. He was cavalier about the difference. "Then we'll just have to be flexible and work something out." I told him our house was on the market and hadn't sold, and he quipped, "Have faith. That's what I did." It seemed to me that it was easy for him to have faith at my expense.

Was I just being obstinate and self-righteous in not wanting to go? Was I just a poor team player? I didn't want to go to this church, but it had been our home church at one time. Our close friends were there, and Becky longed for the comfort of home. Charles said, "What's the problem? It's a great opportunity. You can be bi-vocational, and have the stability you need that way."

My questions had been given pat answers, but I didn't feel satisfied. Under the pressure from all sides, however, I gave in. And we headed back home.

We arrived in St. Louis and I immediately began to observe the routine. In spite of my reservations, I presented myself at my first church service, trying my best to be open-minded. My tolerant nobility (something I've never been medaled for) didn't last long.

The order of worship featured two or three soloists, with the director singing just before the message. This wasn't a worship service, or a praise celebration. It was a competition!

No one here seemed to realize the word "worship" meant to rest. Wounds are healed through rest, not entertainment. And the most profound rest from life's burdens, the sweetest refreshment to carry on another day, comes during the quietness of gazing upon the beauty of the Lord. The sacred was interpreted with entertaining noise. The people needed to worship but they were given a circus instead.

As I set out to turn the tide of worship, I discovered why the music director was the only one to sing in the coveted spot just before the message. He was an integral part of the special effects staging; his song was the dramatic curtain rising on the mighty sermon. The exact atmosphere had to be created, and he was the only one sexy enough to qualify. This rule created two problems.

It turned the worship service into voodoo, and it discouraged others by sorting gifts into a caste system of opportunity. This same spirit of voodoo extended to the realm of public prayer; prayers weren't considered acceptable to God without a form of precise incantation. This was not Christianity. It was superstition. At best, it was entertainment supported by an enlarged ego.

On my first deacon's meeting the pastor reported the gifts to be low and encouraged the deacons to promote the offering at this coming Sunday. And they wanted me to stand up and make a plea for a generous gift. This was not according to the agreement and I refused. But this refusal became the cornerstone of my unfriendly departure. The senior deacon found distaste in the assignment but followed the pastors prompting.

To ad injury to the already tense situation I had to make a smart remark: "I have never heard and announcement that the offerings were so generous that the people could skip a week."

The love offering practice allowed him to preach revivals in other places and tell the host church he lived by faith, without salary. This increased the sympathy of their giving. The Pastor always failed to mention that his home church provided him with a $15,000 benefit package, over and above his weekly love offering.

I was a Preacher of Jesus Christ, to promote their healing." It was my job to extract pain from those who were hurting, and the position required a standup guy. Having started this church position with doubt and trepidation, it became clear, quickly, that the doubt had been well placed. There were huge chasms of difference in my worship philosophy and other areas. These differences would either be reconcilable or irreconcilable. Only time and effort would tell.

Though life during this time was heavy with burden and frustration, one single blessing outweighed all the trials on the other side of the sea-saw. Becky came in one day and said, "The dogs have come home." After thirteen years of marriage, she was carrying our child. (Apparently I was being given opportunity for a "make-up test" in depth of character.) What excitement roared into our home! We could barely wait to get through our long, tough days to talk about baby names. The tender mercies of family life streamed over the desert of our lives with bubbling refreshment.

After many weeks of appropriately solemn consideration, we settled on our choices for the baby's name. For a boy, I chose Joshua. Joshua was a hero of the faith, a man willing to make second efforts. Becky chose Joel Gregory, after a preacher she highly respected. For a girl, I wanted Jennifer, after the character on the television show WKRP in Cincinnati, played by Lonnie Anderson. (I don't remember having a moment's conflict about choosing spiritual-warrior "Joshua" for a boy, and glamour-girl "Jennifer" for a girl.) Becky chose Elayne, after her best friend in seminary.

A protocol was also decided. If the baby was a boy, Becky got to name him. If the baby was a girl, I got to name her. I won. Our daughter's name is Jennifer. But Jennifer was still a package waiting to be delivered when, five months into our church calling, the board of deacons summoned me in for a corrective interview. Without talking in concrete terms, they alluded to discontent. "Exactly what is it you don't like?" I asked. The only thing they seemed to know for sure was that they didn't like the way I made announcements. "What's to be unhappy about? The announcements are brief, and read off the list handed to me. Are announcements supposed to be entertainment? I see, you want Johnny Carson."

After two hours of hide and seek conversation, we got down to the real issue. I said, "Let's see. You are unhappy about my performance.

When I left this church to go to seminary, we had a pre-school department. When I returned, it was gone. Today we have a well furnished department with trained workers. When I left, the church had a discipleship training program; when I came back, it was gone. Tonight, as we sit here wasting time, there are two well-trained people on visitation. I think what's been achieved under my five-month beginning speaks well of my performance. Which part of these changes are you unhappy with?"

There was no response, so I continued. "I don't think you're really unhappy with my performance. I think you're disturbed because I won't use my office to rubber stamp everything the pastor wants. But I was not called here to just serve the pastor's needs or wishes. Nor was I called here to serve just yours. I was called to serve the greater constituency of an entire congregation. The people of this church deserve better care than they are presently receiving. My soul will not rest until I make every effort to struggle for their souls."

The painful part of this meeting was that my closest friends remained mute; they didn't stand up for me. My good friend whom I had just spoken with before the meeting remained quiet and let me bleed to death on ministries battle field. Jesus said, "He who is not for me is against me." There was no neutral ground with Him. My pagan buddies in Vietnam, some of whom I had only known a day, had stood with me under literal gun fire. Why wouldn't my long-time spiritual friends stand with me under the slightest of discomforts? The church battle was over; I resigned under pressure after just nine months. After a spirit is broken, it doesn't take long for the end to come. I had come to help heal a church body. Instead, I had been broken inside. I resigned under the pressure to wander in the wilderness.

The moral of the story: When you are having a nice family gathering and the phone rings, don't answer.

GEORGE P. HUTCHINGS - COMBAT SURVIVAL

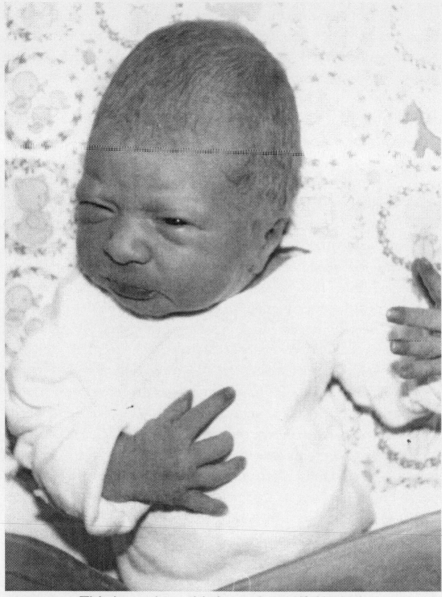

This is no dog - this is our beautiful baby!
After 13 years of marriage, George did not think he was
responsible enough to be a father - so he bought two dogs to see
if he could take care of them - one died and the other ran away.

GEORGE P. HUTCHINGS - COMBAT SURVIVAL

CHAPTER 20
MAN EATER GRACE

In 1982, after leaving the church, the A.B. Dick Company in Kansas City hired me to sell printing presses, so I moved there. Becky stayed with her job in St. Louis because we needed her insurance plan to pay for the baby. After the birth, she would join me, and baby would make three.

Even though I had moved on to another job, I hadn't forgotten the St. Louis church so easily. They may have decided they were finished with me, but I hadn't decided I was finished with them yet. So, every Sunday morning I'd call one of the "lynch mob" to remind them why I was out of ministry work, selling printing presses.

There are names for people like me. The kindest of these names is "jerk." I am certain many folks have purchased tickets to my funeral-probably front row seats so they can spit on my grave.

But, all the bitterness in the world couldn't mar the joy of April 28, 1982, when my phone rang at 4 AM. The baby was coming! On the trip from Kansas City to St. Louis, I passed a cop doing 80 MPH. I guess he figured someone doing 80 in a four-door station wagon must have something pretty important to get to. He didn't pursue. I got to the hospital, and no one in the whole hospital, it seemed, knew where Becky was. Was she dead, alive, or in delivery?

My mind was still clocking 80. I spent more time finding her than I did driving to the hospital. The panic button had been pushed too many times. I tried to calm myself by remembering it took thirteen years for the dogs to come home. A few more minutes wouldn't hurt. But, every uncertain minute felt like eternity.

Finally, a nurse showed me to Becky's room. She was alive, well, and never more beautiful. Then the nurse brought in our new baby. "Oh, no," I gulped. "What have we done? This is a real baby. We have to take care of her for a long time." I was suddenly overwhelmed with fear, and the incalculable weight of such a great responsibility. Send her back and get the dogs! When the first flush of panic was over, I was able to think and see a little more rationally. "Jennifer, you are the plainest baby ever! If you had a cigar, you'd look like Jimmy Durante. Is this the right baby?"

Then Becky handed me our baby girl and I held her for the first time. This was a sacred moment. I know I grew two feet taller right on the spot. Cradled in my arms, I spoke first words to my beautiful, beautiful daughter. "I have a good friend, and Jennifer is her name. I am happy. I am happy. Jennifer is her name." I had never seen such a beautiful baby in all my life! She slobbered all over me. I was thrilled. Just look at that! Doesn't she have the cutest slobber!

My wife and my baby's love helped ease my pain and calm the angry bear in me. And I began to listen again to the distant voice of the Shepherd: "Crying in the wilderness, prepare ye the way of the Lord!" I answered, "Lord, I don't know how or where!"

He said, "Dump your bitterness, follow me back to St. Louis, and I'll give you a ministry." So I called a former employer in St. Louis, and he took me back immediately. I resigned from A.B. Dick, and packed up for St. Louis. Becky passed me on the road going the opposite way to Kansas City, where she finished out my lease there.

We couldn't afford two apartments, and with Becky and Jennifer settled comfortably in the Kansas City apartment, I could get by with a little help from my St. Louis friends. First, Howard and Delores Hale put me up, Semper Fi. Howard and I first met when I was a college freshman. We worked together at J.C. Penney's back when I was a college freshman.

GEORGE P. HUTCHINGS - COMBAT SURVIVAL

I was constantly expressing my new faith to co-workers, but no one would listen. Disgusted with the lack of response, I sat down in the lunchroom one day, beside a man I'd never met before. He said he had just been transferred from Wisconsin. I barked, "Have you found a place to go to church yet?" He replied in the most disarming way, "No, can you suggest a place?"

From that moment on, Howard and I were buddies. We were just what each other needed; he came to my church, and I listened to his "Howles"-my nickname for his roaring bad jokes. Despite his dismal jokes, Howard was (and still is) one of the most gracious, kindhearted men I have ever known. And his wife, Delores, is just as much a treasure. Besides being an accomplished pianist and soprano soloist, she was beautiful, poised, and known for her gracious longsuffering of many "Howie" moments. I never knew if Howard ever served in the Marines, but he had Semper Fi. When I needed help, he took me in. Howard and Delores did not allow me to bleed to death on the battle field of life. I was anxious not to be an imposition on valued friends, so after a while I moved on to the Danniley's.

Down through the years, for some reason we always ran into Carole and Larry Danniley in Penney's stores, either in St. Louis or Ft. Worth. Carole always laughed at my jokes, so that gave this family a favored position in my book. But it was Bootsy and Shotsy who sealed the bonding between our families.

While Larry and I were in seminary in Ft Worth, the Danniley's had a death in the family. Larry and Carol needed to attend the Missouri services. We agreed to watch Bootsy and Shotsy, their two French poodles, in their absence. After all, how much trouble could two little dogs (that barely amounted to a yap at your feet) be? Apparently Larry and Carole hadn't heard about our own two-dog disgrace, so they wantonly abandoned Bootsy and Shotsy with us.

Because our back yard was enclosed with a privacy fence, late one night, we let Bootsy and Shotsy out to run for a while. (I think actually, we were losing enthusiasm for the whole "Go boom boom ritual." They were big boys and could do it on their own.)

When I was ready to go to bed, I stepped out on the patio to call them in. The yard was barren. Pandemonium is the closest adjective to describing what came next. Attired only in my pajamas and with a flashlight sweeping neighborhood hedges, I bolted up and down the streets calling out, "Bootsy! Shotsy!" The neighbor's lights were still on so my plea was in a whispered holler. When a police car turned the corner towards me, there, in its headlights, were the darling little dogs. Sympathizing with my dilemma, the strapping policeman gave chase and caught one of them, while I went another direction after the other one. We met again in the beam of his headlights, each with a catch.

The officer, panting and hatless, dangled his poodle prisoner toward me and asked with a trace of scorn, "Is this the poop or the snot?" I had discovered a new euphemism for when life ran amuck. It could all be summed up with, "Poopsie and snotsie are running loose again."

Shortly after returning to St. Louis in 1983, Richard Judd, a retired preacher and long-time friend traced me from my former church, to Kansas City, and back to Howard Hale. He finally found me at the Dannileys with a proposition. He wanted me to preach at New Hope Church. What an appropriate name for the place of service. And, New Hope Church turned out to be a divine appointment.

Becky, Jennifer, and I rolled onto the parking lot at a corner building. There was no sign indicating that it was a church. Broken Jim Beam bottles littered the asphalt.

There were four men dressed in Army fatigues will long dirty stringy hair standing by the front door.

I told Becky to stay in the car, and then locked the doors. Approaching the men with a big smile, I asked: "Is this New Hope Baptist Church?" They replied, "Yes." "Good, I am to preach here this morning," was my reply. They said, "Good, we are the deacons!"

We hit it off immediately. Soon after, they called me to become their bi-vocational pastor. That means you do the work, but you don't get paid. It didn't matter. I would have paid them to be their pastor.

By that time, the Kansas City lease had finally expired, and Becky was headed home to St. Louis. We had no money, a newborn, and no place to live, but the Dannileys knew of a Catholic priest who had an apartment. He let us live in that apartment for several months and never charged us a cent. Our first Christmas as a family was spent there. It seemed humbly appropriate to be living in a borrowed apartment during that season, mirroring a time when Jesus had no place to lay his head. Jennifer's first Christmas came at a time when her parents didn't have a place to call home. But it was a precious time for family bonding.

Becky and I were listening to the radio one evening while putting up the Christmas tree. Taking a break, I laid down beside Jennifer on the floor, looking into her beautiful, blue eyes. The radio station was playing the song, Man Eater. Just as the song went, "Ho, ho, here she comes, the man eater," Jennifer crawled up and bit me on the nose! We caught it on camera.

So many times in this season of wilderness wandering I'd felt like Satan had been the "man-eater" of my soul, set on the destruction of my spirit and strength.

But I was sustained by a power far greater than any such predators. I had the glorious, restorative encouragement of a resurrected Savior, and the melting, tender love of a man-eater princess. Though at times the struggle seemed viciously tight, there was never really any question about which of the two man-eating forces was victor.

Shortly after Christmas we found a home. And we even made peace with our friends. Becky baked me a humble pie and it choked all the way down, but it became nourishment for a new beginning.

Poopsie and snotsie weren't running loose anymore.

Becky and Jennifer, 1983.

George and his daughter Jennifer loving each other.

Jennifer's highschool graduation - That's my girl!

Randy and Esther Trueblood use their van for a bus ministry.

Jennifer loved Mr. Pig (his real name) at New Hope Baptist.

GEORGE P. HUTCHINGS - COMBAT SURVIVAL

CHAPTER 21
MURDER IN THE MINISTRY

The people of New Hope Church hurt so badly they didn't need to say a word. Fewer than fifteen assembled for worship in this place, but the intensity of their despair felt like the burden of a full stadium. Only a few of these folks were working people. The rest were one step above street people. Most of them didn't have hot and cold running water, so one can imagine the smell. Their former pastor stole money, lied and tried to close the church. They were just one small congregation trying to survive the desperate needs of the larger South St. Louis community in which they lived. Watch out Seminary 101! High ideas and life were just about to have a head-on collision.

Once, when arriving at an apartment building for a pastoral call, a second-floor window slammed open above me, and a mess of belongings crashed onto the street in front of me. A few minutes later, the evictor appeared on the sidewalk with a hammer in hand, and set to work on a car windshield. During intermission, she turned to me. We had never met before, but she knew I was the preacher. Only detectives and preachers wore suits, and since I had not arrested her for hammering out her boyfriend's windshield, that only left one choice.

She cried, "Preacher, you don't know how bad my man is." The next words had to be chosen carefully. Remembering a polite psychology book, my offering was made. "Ma'am, is he really that bad? No one can make you become angry or out of control. You choose to let them." She said, "Darn right! Thank you, preacher!" She turned to the rear window of the car and smashed it out also. Returning to me, she said, "Preacher, you haven't seen my man."

"What does he do? Beat you? Cheat on you? Do drugs?" "Let me show you," she replied, leading me upstairs to introduce us.I said, "Give me the hammer." I should have kept the hammer for the rest of my days in that calling. There were lots of times I could have used it. I remember the cold winter Sunday morning when some hoods came in during the worship service and stole my poor people's coats. We had to start locking the doors behind us. But for every grievous time at New Hope, there were dozens of sweet times. Randy and Ester Trueblood, a couple in their seventies, were one of the few families in the church with a running vehicle, so they made their "church bus" rounds in a well-aged van.

Most of the church gathered and dispersed by way of the Trueblood shuttle. This created a close family unity, with the Truebloods taking care of what we called their grandchildren.

There was a spirit of wide-eyed fun and expectation those days. We were so weak we had to depend on the Lord for everything. There was a piano and an organ, but no one could play them, so each week we even had to pray for a pianist. Delores Hale often came to play. When she couldn't, Randy Trueblood would lead the music.

Wednesday night, when we took prayer requests from one another, was the sweetest fellowship. People were hurting, and this church was their only hope things would ever be better. Typical prayer requests were for food, rent money, utility bills to be paid, someone to get out of jail, and clothes for the winter. Every Sunday, as a follow-up to Wednesday's requests, people told of answered prayers.

Once an 80-year-old woman, Mrs. Howard, testified she had received a can of beans and had shared it with her neighbor. The Lord had put me in a small church of hurting people. His providence in the calling was, as always, divinely timely.

These people were broken, but they deserved respect. I had been given just the right place to pour out my heart in service. They didn't care who sang just before the sermon, or how I made my announcements.

This was a time for healing for all of us, me first. Slowly, our numbers grew to 148 as our love abounded. Some former members came back, including Ed Ham, Jr., who played the piano. Although the church had been on the brink of default when we arrived, after only a few weeks, we started making our budget. From then on, we were never late on a building payment, and they have since paid off all debts.

Big stories became entertainment. Ray and Ellen Ham returned to be members of our church as a new burst of life. Ray was a character and always carried a smile. So I tested him.

Ray, did you ever fish the Gasconade River? He said, "No." Then my reply came like this: "The Gasconade is a clear river with some depth. Some friends of mine took me fishing in a light weight John boat and the biggest fish I had ever caught was a perch. They were talking about 18 pound stripped bass! Well, I hooked a big fish. Would you believe that fish pulled the boat up the stream and then back down. Finally, the fish went straight down and I was afraid to pull the line to tight or it would break. I wanted that fish! So I stripped down and had my friend hold the rod while I would swim hand over hand down the line. When I reached the bottom the fish had swum into an old car and the line was wrapped around a spring underneath the front seat."

In my mind I said to this fish that I am coming in there to get you. Ray you will never believe what that fish did, "He rolled the window up and popped the clutch." Ray came to church but didn't speak for six months.

The relationships become a profound part of who we are, are almost always an intermingling of joy and tragedy. This is how we remember New Hope. And no tragedy was worse than what happened to our beloved, thirteen-year-old Rose. When she was murdered by her mother's live-in boyfriend, we were stunned. We had been successful at pressing for Rose and her siblings to be moved to a foster home, but the system had returned them to their mother without our knowledge. Innocent, Rose had been raped and then shot with a deer rifle. Her family didn't even give her a funeral, so our church held a memorial service.

Delicate words had to be chosen, words of weight. Souls needed more than pat answers. A person's life deserved purpose. How could a loving God let this happen?

The only answer was that Jesus was stronger in death than He was in life. Rose was desecrated by her own family; Jesus was betrayed by his own disciple. She had her Larry; Christ had his Judas. Both lives ended brutally, but both deaths had dignity because there was a God who cared. She was in divine company. She had gone into the loving arms of one who had chosen to suffer and endure every pain that would ever fall upon any of His precious children, including Rose.

He had done it so Rose could come home to Him. New Hope Church offered just what it said. We bonded, taking care of one another,

"Having all things common." Amen.

The depression that followed Rose's murder was profound. But, in His sweet provision, the Lord sent us water even during those desert days. He sent us Jim Bender and Dan Fuller as volunteer youth ministers.

When they called to inquire about the possibility of such service, I arranged a meeting with them first. I arrived in a suit, and they in their jeans. We sat down to talk. My primary issue of concern was why they wanted to work together. Usually a church has only one youth minister. It was refreshing to get some help, and the more the better if it came in dozens, but caution had to be exercised in a church that had already taken far more than its share of battering.

After the interview, I found the young men to be something extraordinary: a pure gift from God, no trickery involved. Our fine young men eventually went to Bible College. Joy came to our hearts when the church helped Jim raise $2,000 to support an evangelistic trip to South America. He came back with a report of 500 decisions for Christ. Dan Fuller took a lot of ribbing from his proud-as-papa church family after being named Hannibal LaGrange College Man of the Year.

When one invests his life in the lives of others, it brings marrow to the bone to see them do well. A student exceeding the teacher is the teacher's highest compliment.Despite its battered appearance and grand-canyon needs, tiny little New Hope congregation in South St. Louis had managed to pull its self up out of the dust to send waves of love around the world, through its own community, and down to the bones of its very own minister. To use a sports metaphor, it was the World Series, bottom of the ninth, two outs, and one run down, one man on base. And this small unsightly group of believers hit a home run. The roar of cheering will never stop.

Break open the grape juice.

CHAPTER 22
LITTLE FOXES THAT HURT

"Little Foxes that Hurt" is a Bible reference for small things that cause immeasurable damage, one bit at a time. In the analogy, rather than tearing up the vine with one fell attack, the fox nips at it, bleeding it subtly and slyly. The Fox knows not to, "Kill the goose that laid the golden egg."

Ransom for Red Chief

It seems every church has a, "Ransom for Red Chief" character. The short story is about a red headed rascal that was always in trouble. One day two kidnappers took the boy but then paid the parents to take him back!

My Red Chief was about 12 years old and could not sit still during a worship service. He had the weakest bladder west of the Mississippi. He was always up and going. My favorite antic was when he was selling candy as a fund raiser for his school. I asked, "Now do I pay for this now or when I get the candy?" He said, "Oh, now of course! I knew I would never see the candy, and I didn't. It didn't matter, the kid needed a little spending money and he earned it with the entertainment he provided.

Dooms Day hit! Red Chief was sodomized by two men. He told me of how they forced him into their car, and later tied his hands to a bedpost. It broke my heart. Our prize young man violated, this was an outrage! The police didn't seem interested, so I began my own investigation, but his parents sent word not to follow up. They were challenged with Down syndrome and couldn't protect themselves.

As a fox usually does, these men had come and gone without identification. A community activation group, called ACORN wanted to help us picket the prime supplier of pornography in our area, a local drug store. Since pornography had been an issue in our young man's assault, New Hope took on the cause whole-heartily. Even Mrs. Howard, at 80 years of age, came out and carried a sign. Our vice was not yet dead.

But how could we persuade the owner of this drug store to give up a portion of his profits? We knew the picketing wouldn't be enough. All he would have to do was wait us out until we got tired of pestering him. When I discovered the owner was Jewish, I decided to appeal to him through his religious heritage. So, while those who picketed sat in front of the door, I began to preach a sermon. Through the glass I could see the owner who had summed me up as some foolish street preacher who would annoy him and then go away. We established eye contact and the one who looked away first lost. It was time to play my hand.

Had this been poker, the owner would have held a pair: air conditioning and the street heat. I held three of a kind: the teaching of a Good Shepherd (who lays down his life for his friends-and in my mind, this was for all the chips); the teaching of the store owner's religious heritage (Abraham and Moses were on, my side); and a sermon God had put on my heart.

Looking the man straight in the eye I said, "This one who claims the honor of being a Jew is not living as a Jew at all. God called the Jews, through Abraham, to come away from the pagan practices of the Gentiles; this man is thriving on the pagan practices of the Gentiles. God gave the Jews, through Moses, His Law. "Thou shall not commit adultery," this man peddles adultery.

And God gave the Jews through Paul, elite among Jews, a warning: "Not everyone of the race is a child of God in his heart."

GEORGE P. HUTCHINGS - COMBAT SURVIVAL

This man does not have the God of the Jews in his heart.

"This pharmacy is not for the healing of the community, but for the harm. It is a front for selling smut. Judas made money by selling an innocent man for thirty pieces of silver. How much does this owner get for selling the safety and dignity of others' souls?"

"When Jesus hung on the cross they 'pulled his garment from him' to bring shame. All of us know a person's body is sacred. This man knows it just as we do. Yet he chooses to participate in the shame of others."

The owner moved the magazines behind the counter. It wasn't all we had asked for, but we settled. The fox had been confronted and a small victory had been won. To show our good faith and desire for healing, we then entered the store to buy things. Sometimes when you win any sort of victory against an enemy, a host of new ones come to take its place like the mythological characters that grow back three heads for every one you lop off. The pack of foxes was growing in my own life at an alarming rate.

The Thirsty Fox

With all our moves, Becky and I still hadn't sold the house in Texas. Finally after two years of paying double house payments, it sold with a $20,000 loss in equity. It is funny how preachers can have faith at my expense. On the heels of that devastating financial loss, we were ripe for Mr. Sydney O'koye from Nigeria to come into our lives.

He had married an American woman who worked with Becky. We all became good friends. Sydney wanted me to become an investor in his import/export business and it seemed like a very promising opportunity. So, to test the waters, I borrowed $5000 to invest in a shipment of sugar to Nigeria. Syd came back after the shipment was completed and paid off as promised.

He asked if I wanted to do it again, but this time with $10,000. I borrowed the $10,000 and Rich Kim, encouraged by my first success, borrowed $5,000 to buy in, too. He also traveled with Syd to accompany our profits home.

A month later Rich returned with no money. The man guarding the plane before departure from Nigeria had informed Rich his papers weren't in order. Rich asked, "What will it take to make them in order?"

The guard with the machine gun said, "$500."

Rich handed over the money and felt lucky to come home with his life. Ten years later I owed $13,000 on the $10,000 I borrowed, and Rich's debt still wasn't paid. This fox almost killed the vine. I knew I never wanted to go to Africa!

The Funny Fox

A long time friend and co-worker, Gordon Mauck, wanted to introduce me to the insurance business. He was a great guy, but could never hold a job, so I wasn't interested in anything he was proposing. He hounded me, however, until I finally gave in and made an appointment to see Dan Kim, Sales Manager.

The first thing I said to Mr. Kim was "I'm only here for Gordon's sake; I'm not really interested."

"That's funny," he replied. "Since he was the one who made the recommendation, I wasn't interested in you." We had a good laugh and that began a whole new course of events.

"Since I'm here," I asked, "tell me why I should be interested in insurance." He put the case before me, and when the right time came for a career change, Dan Kim hired me and Rick Kim trained me.

GEORGE P. HUTCHINGS - COMBAT SURVIVAL

That first year with the company, Rich helped me write a year's quota in six months. The payoff was a trip to Palm Springs. We worked hard, and we played hard. We won five consecutive convention trips. Rich wasn't just someone to work with; he was a brother. Now I was working 40 plus hours in the insurance business while being the pastor of a people who needed me for another 40 plus hours.

Gordon did me the best favor possible. He introduced me to Rich Kim. Rich and I have worked, played, and covered one another back ever since. Thanks Gordon, you did good.

The Fox that Dies

Mrs. Martin was one of New Hope's challenges. I knew she was a person in pain from our first meeting, and during my entire four years as her pastor, I seldom saw her smile. Each time we met I gave her a hug to try to make her smile, but the smile seldom came. She was a soul under torment of nipping, relentless pain, but she never asked for, or expected, help.

One Sunday I moved over to Mrs. Martin and pointed to the other side of the church asking who a certain individual was. When she turned her head, I kissed her on the cheek and she laughed saying, "Oh! You, you always make me smile." I won.

Mrs. Martin had a daughter in the occult that would call regularly and threaten to kill her. One day she gutted a cat, put the cat's blood on the porch. We were all relieved when the daughter moved to Florida, hoping the mental torment of her "nipping" was over.

One Sunday Mrs. Martin came to church crying. Two boys had moved in down the street had stolen her Social Security check. The police didn't seem to care. The sharp nip of her foxes tormented me again.

Mrs. Martin had experienced enough pain, and I wasn't going to stand by watching my friend bleed to death on the battle field.

In my suit and tie, and holding a five D-cell battery flashlight, one night I watched the boy's house until both had arrived home. The boys were both home and on drugs. I stepped to the door with the flashlight resting on my shoulder. I knocked. When one of the boys answered, I shined the light in his eyes and slammed the flash light across his forehead knocking him down. The other boy cowered in the corner.

I picked the boy up and said, "Take a look at my face. Do you know who I am?"
"No!" He cried.

"I'm the preacher from the corner church and right now I think I'm Clint Eastwood. You stole Mrs. Martin's check." I dropped him to the floor and then picked him back up. "I want Mrs. Martin's check now!" He quickly handed over the check, to which I responded "You will never hurt another one of my people, and you will be gone by morning."

I walked to the door, turned around, and looked at the two gaping, stunned faces. I said, "A benediction is in order. Dearly beloved, we gather here together in the sight of God and in the presence of these vermin from the pit of hell. It is hoped, dear Lord, that they will soon be returned to the place of their origin. We humbly bow our heads and request the same pit of hell for their children and for the children's children to the third and forth generation. In Jesus name, Amen."

At 10:00 AM the next morning I checked on the two and they had moved, never to be seen by us again. Mrs. Martin and I were going over the edge together. One night Mrs. Martin called.

A nurse from a Tampa hospital had called to tell her that her daughter was dead, and Mrs. Martin was receiving calls from her dead daughter. Mrs. Martin was raving in pain. I arrived at Mrs. Martin's home by 9:00 PM. The phone number the nurse had left was for a hospital, but that hospital adamantly denied any record of her daughter's admittance or death. As her pastor, I requested her Bible. It was worn from being carried but the yellow pages indicated it had never been read. Mrs. Martin had gone to church every Sunday but only engaged in an empty ritual. She had never read her book or entered into worship. The scripture, "Absent from the body, present with the Lord," meant nothing to her. When people die they either go to heaven or hell but they don't make phone calls.

Mrs. Martin was living out the verse from Matthew, "Rachel weeping for her children, but could not be comforted because there were not."

We eventually called every hospital in Tampa, as well as the police and the morgue. No luck. I knew the daughter wasn't dead; this was just another ungodly trick. Watching Mrs. Martin's turmoil was emotionally horrendous. I could see she was going over the edge in sanity. (I'm reminded of a bumper sticker that read, 'Humpty Dumpy was Pushed.' Mrs. Marin would agree.)

Some time after midnight I offered my best pastoral prayer. On my way out of her home that night, I looked back to see Mrs. Martin sitting, weeping with her head in her hands. With the aid of her pastor and friend, the scripture, and prayer, "She could not be comforted." That night Mrs. Martin died of heart failure and I entered Missouri Baptist Hospital for a three year stay due to a nervous breakdown.

After three years of hospitalization and eighty-seven electric shock treatments, I returned home. My daughter came to give me a hug and I didn't know her name.

George starting Eagle Wing Ministries, 1994.

GEORGE P. HUTCHINGS - COMBAT SURVIVAL

CHAPTER 23
"ARE THESE THE GOODIES?" OR
"A MASSIVE PITY PARTY!"

Depression and problems are not the same thing. Problems can be solved with reason and action. Depression comes without rhyme or reason and leaves in much the same way. People suffering from manic depression have huge mood swings. This had been a way of life for me, but my youth had always been there to pick me up. This time the wellsprings of youth were gone, and I was long overdue for a diagnosis and plan of treatment.

During three year stay at the hospital, Dr. Wilber Gearhart administered 88 electric shock treatments for the depression and tried every possible combination of lithium and other drugs to balance my blood chemistry. Finally the formula started coming together, but it was unclear if I was strong enough to resume regular life. In January 1989, Becky brought me home from the hospital, but the doctor, fearing I might still hurt myself, requested round-the-clock surveillance. So, I came home to find a watch care squad of men from our church, Jess Nance, Gervis Moore, and Tom Coleman.

Quite rapidly, my memory began to come back, and journaling became my habit. I had to write down my memories in order to discover who was in this body. Still being incoherent and my condition unknown to many friends, Garden Baptist Church actually called asking me to preach a sermon. It was difficult to put my thoughts together, but I agreed. It was a fortuitous experience because it was the deaf congregation that needed a preacher.

It only took one look at the congregation and I knew I had no right to speak to them because I knew nothing about deafness.

GEORGE P. HUTCHINGS - COMBAT SURVIVAL

I told them so, and said that I had also been a person of pain and that I would just tell my story. They cried, I cried and they said that I could be their preacher until they found a deaf preacher. Then they didn't look any further and for five years, I was the pastor of the deaf church.

The people were marvelous in teaching me sign language. They often taught me the wrong signs so they could laugh at me. Dan Gruchalla taught me the sign for gay instead of the word Gospel. So in the middle of a sermon, I used the sign gay for Gospel and they all broke out laughing and I had no idea what I said.

Dan became a great friend. He was the music director and was the first to begin teaching sign language.

March 18, 1968, George was wounded in Vietnam and it became his day of pain. March 18, 2006, Jennifer and Nick without collaboration, got married and it turned into a day of joy!

GEORGE P. HUTCHINGS - COMBAT SURVIVAL

Dan is short, heavy, bald, and wears thick glasses. The first thing he taught me to say in sign was, "It is always fun to flirt with beautiful women." I think he was trying to get me in trouble.

Dan is still my friend but I never mastered sign language. My ability is limited but I know enough to enjoy singing in sign. When I sing people cry, and not because they are having a religious experience. One day a lady handed me the hymn book and I began to sing. She looked and me and retrieved the hymnal. Then one day I was singing in sign the wonderful hymns of the faith and Dan came over and folded my arms. I can't sing on key even in sign language.

But the emptiness in my soul was unabated. I remember watching a movie, Papillion, starring Steve McQueen. Papillion was a gangster who was arrested for the wrong crime. He spent the rest of his life in jail, with everyone expecting him to break out. The last scene shows him lying on the floor, either going into a dream, or dying. He is taken up before a great light and says, "You of all people know that I am innocent of this crime."

A deep, authoritative voice returns, "It is not for the crime I hold you guilty. I hold you guilty of a wasted life."

Was this the story of my life, too? Now forty years old, had I wasted my life on college, seminary, one of the most difficult churches in history, and a few other imperfections? I'd studied, sacrificed, worked, and gotten in return a broken mind and body. I didn't even know my daughters name. Are these the goodies, I was promised when I set out to follow you, Lord?

The answer that came back from Providence served notice on my soul. He wanted a man who for no earthly good would serve Him. My bitterness over failure indicated I had been working for something in return: pride.

And my greatest fear had come upon me, failure. In the sight of my peers, I had failed.

It seemed to always be my destiny to fail and be laughed at, yet "I knew that my redeemer lives." How then was I to live? What if I were to just accept my fate, and trust the Lord to act on my best behalf: What if I just accepted humiliation with good grace. Could I accept, with good grace, that I was not ever going to be the popular guy on the block? I was never going to be the most successful guy, the most charismatic guy. That I would never be validated by my peers? Is my destiny to be one of rejection by everyone except my Lord? If so then I would have to learn to draw my self esteem from Him because no one else can validate.

I slept for a while and then awoke with a verse in mind: "They who wait upon the Lord shall renew their strength. They shall mount up their wings as eagles' wings. They shall run and not be weary. They shall walk and not faint."

Renewed strength! But before that strength arrived, "I would wait."

I had never done that before-wait. I had always been running, pursuing, fighting. It was time to wait for the winds of Providence. Broken and beaten, I decided to stop fighting for what I thought I deserved, and I decided to stop trying to invent an image that would impress others. I decided to just wait on the Lord. And, for the first time, I felt the peace of such a release. I would wait to see what the winds of Providence would bring.

In the movie, "The Right Stuff" Gus Grissom panicked as the space capsule fell into the sea. He blew the door open prematurely and the astronauts were rescued but the capsule was lost. The prior astronauts had all gone to the White House and met with President and Mrs. Kennedy.

Mrs. Grissom opens her refrigerator that is stocked with food and beer. She laments, "Are these the goodies?"

That is the question many people ask themselves. After a life of sacrifice, hard work and sweat; is this all I get? "No trip to the White House? No Jackie?" Somehow, in the Christian life we believe that if we do everything right we will be rewarded here and now.

My pastor had preached many times that Christians live a sacrificial life. The sacrificial life is to follow the invisible spirit of a living God. My pastors forgot to tell me one thing, "Count the cost." Because the minute you go out and follow God, the pastors help ceases. You are on your own. It was 1998 and John Kihumba was a member of our church but his two year old son, Alexam had not yet joined the family. The American Embassy in Nairobi, Kenya had been bombed. John and I had a panic, how to get Alexam to America. We hustled up a golf tournament. I invited our pastor to play. The tournament only cost $100 per person, but he said he didn't play golf. He knew what we were doing but did not even give an offering. But he played one month later in the church tournament.

I asked the minister of youth to play and he said he never paid $100 to play golf. I said, 'It is a fund raiser to bring Alexam home." The man was adamant, no!

These men were not poor. The pastor lived in a mansion in West County St. Louis and the minister of youth was making $50,000 per year. But their hearts were cold and I learned to hold these men in disrespect. It was a hard lesson for me to learn but no matter how critical or raw the cause; my closest friends cannot be expected to accept the calling that is sat before me. Alexam was my calling, not theirs. I would have to work it out between me and the one calling me to the task.

This was the beginning of what I call my "wilderness years." If I was to learn to "Wait for renewed strength," life would deliver lessons in practical waiting. In the middle of the fight the Christian leaders could not be found. Every thing I had learned in life was that you never allow your men to bleed to death on the battle field. The "Christian leaders" did not respond to help a member of their church bring a two year old from Africa. They left me hanging. Thank God the church members, people of faith from opposing theological positions, and non-believers could see the impending danger. They came from unexpected places and pitched their tent towards Nairobi, Kenya.

We got the boy home. But I stumbled. I hated preachers and called them cowards. Preachers are the men with no guts. They call you out to do a job and then refuse to stand with you. In my mind, "These Men of God," should have been leading the way. Bitterness swept through my heart robbing me of the joy of victory.

I had to ask myself the question: After 35 years of ministry is this the respect I get? A broken body, a mental breakdown, financial disaster, and the people I thought were my colleagues let me die. Are these the goodies of following Christ?

"Waiting for renewed strength," would take practice, practice, practice. I threw out all my books including my Bible. I threw away my calling and addressed my preacher face to face calling him names not to be used in polite company. This was a lesson that I failed miserably. Having a divine temper tantrum was like a two year old throwing a pillow at big daddy. The verse, "God is long suffering towards us not willing that any should perish but have everlasting life" took on new meaning.

The Lord honored my preaching and teaching. He blessed my ministry through unexpected people. But I was "sour grapes" and life was without joy.

It was at this time I understood that churches have their own agenda and there was, "no room in the inn for me." I would go to the people.

It took a long time before I could see my own short comings and understand that if I wanted redemption, I must give redemption. The hardest lesson I had learned was that we do not trust in man but in God. When there is no visible means of support it is easy to point to the men that fail my expectations and hard to trust in an invisible God.

I now feel indebtedness to those who disappointed me. Without them I would never know the freedom of walking with God. This walking with God is new to me because I have always had a job and steady source of income. But in this ministry, how we pay the bills each month is a surprise. The path of this journey has not been perfected but I am learning the joy of a whole new dimension of life.

The past is gone, nothing can be done. The future is not here, nothing can be done. I have today, this moment. I make a deliberate choice to refer all matters to the Almighty. There is no time for self pity; the ball has been tipped, the game is in play, and I run until my time runs out. The Apostle Paul said, "Run the race, finish the course, and keep the faith." I am now in old age and I am running for my finish line without being encumbered by the bitterness that had besieged me.

On Operation Medina one Marine was wounded and began a pity party. The corpsman gave the standard drill instructor reply, "If you want sympathy you are at the wrong place. Sympathy is in the dictionary between shit and syphilis." The Marine responded by picking up his M 16 with his good hand. He continued to fight. The ministry is no place for weakness; we are to fight the "Good fight."

Each year I buy Jennifer a nice piece of jewelry for Christmas. Kansas City was my destination when a call from Becky came. Our foster daughter had stolen all the jewelry given to Jennifer. Jennifer took the phone and in tears told me what happened. I told her, "Jennifer, we are Christian people who lay up for ourselves treasure in Heaven where thief cannot break through and steal, for where your treasure is the will your heart be also." It is just stuff; we look to Heaven for our eternal reward. She said, "Okay." And that was the end of it. We trusted in God and it was liberating.

"Are these the goodies?" Yes, the freedom of living without attachment to this world while depending on a Holy God to work on our best behalf. Yes, these are goodies. The honor of fighting not like a U.S. Marine, but as a Christian soldier fighting back not evil for evil but meeting evil with good. (Matthew chapter 5)

To all those preachers I called SOB's, I can't remember your names. Remember my Christmas motto: "May all my enemies go to Hell, Noel, Noel, Noel, and Noel." I didn't want to sound pious and the chapter needed a bit of earthen wit. This is my way of saying, "If you want sympathy, you are in the wrong place."

CHAPTER 24
THE RUSSIAN GIRLS

In 1990, Kolamkas and Zarnar were the first Russian students at Missouri Baptist College. They were from the Russian Country of Kazakhsan. Kazakhsan is the home of the first Russian astronaut and the country where most of the plutonium is stored.

Missouri Baptist College sits in West St. Louis County far from all the sites of the city. The girls were exchange students and spend their first semester confined to the college campus. Their semester was to expire in two weeks and they would be back to Kazakhsan without having seen the sites and sounds of the city. But most of all they had not had an exchange with faith families.

The College staff became aware of this missed opportunity and I spear headed the drive to raise funds for an extra semester. The Kazakhsan government required that if their tuition was paid in full, they could stay another semester. Immediately, my family became the host family and the girls spent Thanksgiving and Christmas in our home.

The fund raising calls were made, letters written and you know what happened, nothing. It was the night before they were to return home and I told them to go back to their dorm room and pray to Jesus that they experience a resurrection. Kolamkos said, "Mr. Hutchings, you are a very funny man."

Dr. Hewitt, was the President of Missouri Baptist College (MBC) and I explained the situation. He stamped the papers paid-in-full with my promise to raise the funds after the fact.

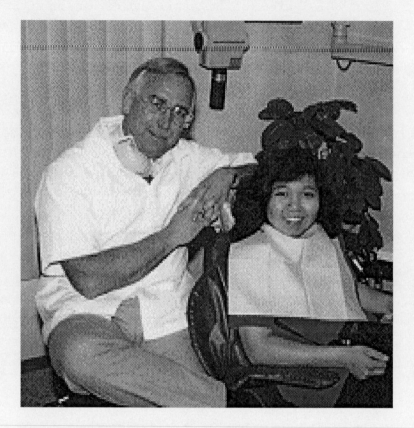

Dr. Gil Hart giving dental care to Kolamkos.

The next morning I broke the news to the girls. I said, "Girls, just as Jesus came out of his tomb to live a new life, you are now leaving your tomb (the dorm room) and have another semester. They laughed and cried and Kolamkos said, "Mr. Hutchings you are a very funny man."

Kolamkas's mother was a university teacher of atheism and was an interpreter for the Russian government. Zarnar's father was the Vice-President of the National Academy of Science. He was also a newly elected member of parliament. The families had been communists and trained atheists.

My pitch to churches was that of a cultural exchange. The girls would tell their stories and sing their Mongolian songs. The churches could accept the girls demonstrating that Christians can love people other than themselves. And the churches, especially Starling Road Baptist Church, gave offerings and took them in with gracious hospitality. Kolamkas and Zarnar could see and feel the love of faith people.

The money for the dorm and tuition came from contributions from church receptions. The needed money was raised in 30 days and another semester was made possible by faith people.

As Kolamkas ate a McDonald hamburger she winced in pain. Oh, no! Another problem. There was no more money to be found for a dentist, but I had a life insurance policy on my mother-in-law. No I didn't kill my mother-in-law, but took the $400 of cash value to Dr. Gil Hart and said, "Take it as far as it will go."

Dr. Hart reported that many teeth were bad. The Russian dentist had only filled in the cavities. In a few years, she would have no teeth. The bill would be $3500 to $4000.

Dr. Hart (a Christian dentist and friend) heard my deep sign and replied with beautiful words, "Don't worry, I'll take care of it." Of course, he kept the $400.

When Kolamkas and Zahar did return to Russia, it was with an overwhelming sense of Christian love. Kolamkas wanted to go home with a color television. She would need one to fit the electric current back home that was 220, I could not the item. I used one a crayons from my daughter's collection and drew a picture of a color television. Kolamka said, "What is this?" I said Kolamkas this is a color television, you take it home and hang in on the wall and one day it will turn into a television set." She Said, "Mr. Hutchings, you are a very funny man."

I was invited by the vice president of the National Institute of Science (Zahar's father) to assist in a scientific experiment. The experiment was a ruse to allow my admittance to Russia. He wanted to give proper thanks because I helped his daughter.

The invitation came to my office at MBC. I muttered to myself $3,000. Immediately, I took the invitation to Dr. Hindson the vice-president and told him what I had. He asked if I was going. I said, "Of course, but I don't know where I will get $3,000."

The walls at Missouri Baptist College are paper thin. A blind student, David Love, two doors down overheard the conversation. The next day David entered my office and asked, "George, are you still going to Russia?" My reply was, "Yes." David then dropped the bomb, "George can I go with you?" Wow, now $3000 was turned into $6000. I said, David if God can give me $3000 he has another $3000 for you." David said, "Good, my mom said that if you would take me, she would pay the way!"

Zahar's father announced that he wanted to take us to meet some of his friends. I didn't know he was taking us to Parliament, but told David that we had better dress up. We donned our suit and ties and followed the man to a huge building. Parliament was out of session but received us in an overflow room for a meet and greet.

Everyone was Dr. Chemistry, Dr. Biology, Dr. Math etc. and I am asking myself, what do I have to tell these men. Then I was introduced as a war hero from Vietnam. That was all I needed, a point of contact. I knew they would regard Americans as proud, arrogant, and self-centered.

I began my discourse with, "I am a sinful man who lives in a nation of many sins. The Vietnam War was one of those sins. We found that just because you put a uniform on a man it does not make the man a soldier in his heart." I am a solider now, but a soldier of the army of Faith. I no longer carry an M16 but I carry a heart of love for all nations. And it is from this background that I became friends with Zahar.

One of the men told me they had found the same thing in Afghanistan. To put a uniform on a man does not make him a soldier, a soldier is something that comes from the heart.

Many questions were asked and the sessions were a success. Many people quietly told me that they too were Christians. A luncheon was scheduled at a local watering hold but the people making the reservations returned stating we not go because their were pistol packing nomads from Afghanistan .We skipped lunch.

It was time for David and me to spend some time with Kolamkos's family. On the way I noticed an open market that had a color television. I bought it and now carried my luggage, David on my arm, and the television on my shoulder.

We walked up the four flights of stairs and knocked on the door. Kolamkos answered and I handed her the television. She said, "Mr. Hutchings, you are a very funny man." I said, "Kolamkos, not do you believe that the invisible can become visible and the impossible become possible?" She said, 90%.

The last night was a huge party, lots of vodka. This was a one time experience and I felt like I must give a Christian thought, something for them to think about. I began, "Mr. Math, when your equation is properly laid out and the formula followed you to receive a correct answer; but if the equation has an error nothing works." He replied, "Correct."

Mr. Biology, you use chemistry that is based on mathematical formulas and in your field when a correct formula is tied to a correct mathematical equation everything cooks. He said, "That is correct."

My argument continued to other fields of science. The point being that when truth is discovered it will work with other fields of science. Truth, we search for truth. Then the things we discover are not invented, the truth was there and we discovered it. That must mean that someone preceded us laying out the axioms of the universe so that man can work hand in hand with truth.

Now my question is this: If truth precedes us and we discover it and not invent it, can truth be personified. And can that personification be Jesus Christ because he said, "I am the truth..." And he rose from the dead proving that what he taught was the truth.

My host coughed up his vodka and said, "I told him I was a Marxist." I fumbled and said, well it was a new thought and may have a weakness on some side, and then of course there is the drink. All was forgiven but the message was received.

GEORGE P. HUTCHINGS - COMBAT SURVIVAL

Kolamkas was there and she made a toast. All of her friends, teachers (Muslims), and family were there. She stood to toast and said, "Since the beginning of my stay at Missouri Baptist College, I began to feel the love and warmth of Christian people for a Muslim girl. They did not make me empty promises. They loved me by helping me. These strangers listened to my Angolan songs, became my friends, and paid my way through school."

And today, something very strange has happened in my heart. I now have the ability to believe 100% in Jesus Christ the Almighty God." Kolamkas later married a military man who read the scriptures in Russian provided by Missouri Baptist and embraced the Christian faith. Currently, Kolamkas works as the interpreter for the American Embassy.

"And now for the rest of the story:"

David and I were in the London airport. We were laden with luggage, David on my right arm with his white cane, and I being very hard of hearing could not understand the audio announcements. We were tripping over each other as we headed for the ticket counter. The attendant welcomed me and I said, "My friend is blind, and I am deaf, but if you speak slowly, I can read your lips.

Immediately the attendant called for help and people came from many directions took our luggage and lead us to a special sitting area. Wow! I needed the help.

Once on the plane the earphones for movie watching were passed out. The flight attendant handed one to David and then looked at me and said, "Oh! You don't need one!"

Irena Salaban - a woman without a country

CHAPTER 25
CLASS ROOM CALAMITY
IRENA SALABAN
"WOMAN WITHOUT A COUNTRY"

It was 1994 and Missouri Baptist University was sending professors to, "The Riga International Bible Institute," Riga Latvia. The religion professors had all made trips and they needed another teacher. I was working part time raising funds for the development department but had the seminary degree necessary to teach.

When the school asked me to teach for ten days in what was once part of Russia, I said yes! The only advice given by previous professors was to position myself in such a manner that students could not ask me to bring them home. Upon arrival, I expected a dignitary from the school to meet me at the airport. But no one was there to pick me up. I just sat and thought. I'm a long way from home....

About 45 minutes later a lady entered the lobby and asked if I was Mr. Hatchings. Close enough, "I am" was the reply. She took me to her husband Gennady Zavaly the President and Founder of the school. I stayed with them the night and school started the next day.

My brief case of books was about four sizes that of a normal book bag. I exaggerated my motions, pretending the bag was heavy, carrying it up the four levels of stairs to the class room. Students offered to carry it but no! This was my special bag. One step at a time I rested the bag on the next step making my awkward way up the winding steps. The students begged to help, but no. This was my special bag of books.

Upon arriving before the class, I used both hands to lift the bag onto the desk. "This is going to be a concentrated time of study;" then I opened the mystery box and pick up a hand full of mini packed M&M's; but it is going to be a sweet day." I threw several students packages of M&M's. They laughed and class began. It became my habit that when a student asked a good question or gave a good answer they would find a package of M&M's flying their way. The week was a success.

My Baltic residence was with a man named Socia. He had been in Germany's concentration camp, and then spent the remainder of his life under Communism. He was not allowed to express his Christian faith. After a week of my stay, Socia took me to a back room and removed some boards from the floor. He showed me his Bible, almost every verse was underlined. This book had been read.

He then pulled an iron craft from the hidden space. It was forged iron in the shape of a heart. A cross spanned the heart and then there was barbed wire around it. He told me it meant that barbed wire cannot keep Christ out of the heart. Then he laid the bomb: But bitterness will. I asked if I could keep the treasures and he granted my wish.

On Wednesday night, Gennady had arranged for me to preach. Then I was told that I was to preach after the "Billy Graham of Russia." The church building was unusual. We met in a gymnasium that featured a basketball court complete with scoreboard. The scoreboard reflected the score as home 1 visitors 0.

I asked about the history of the building. In 1920 a preacher wanted to build a church where all people could worship. The preacher named the church Salvation Temple. He had no money and asked people to donate a brick or the price of a brick.

Socia, who had survived Hitler's concentration camps, forged
this emblem of a heart, cross and barbed wire.

The preacher wrote letters and took out ads in the newspaper;
people laughed. But they brought bricks to the location just to watch
what was happening.

The church was completed and then Russia took over the
country. The church was seized and turned into a basketball arena. It
was now 70 years later and Gennady walked to the church and
demanded the officer in charge give him the keys. All private property
was to be return to the populace. The officer laughed. But everyday
Gennady Zavaly, a small framed man, returned to demand the keys;
the changing political climate scared the officer. One morning the
officer turned the keys over to Pastor Zavaly and said, "You win."

GEORGE P. HUTCHINGS - COMBAT SURVIVAL

The furnace had been destroyed and our prayers could be seen lifted up on our breath. The people crowded together to drawl warmth from one another. The building was packed and I realized I had never before witnessed the fervor of prayers.

It was winter time and a man converted to Christianity. He wanted to be baptized. Gennady said, "The River is frozen, wait until summer." The man insisted upon being baptized and The Pastor asked, "We have to chop a hole in the ice, are you not afraid of the cold?" The man replied, "The cold is nothing, I am afraid of the Hell." The man's theology may not have been the best; but the man's faith could not be denied. The hole was chopped and the man baptized.

Pictures\Scanned Pictures\Monday, November 06, 2006.jpg Picture caption: George and Gennady working together for a furnace. The cold church was more than prayers could sustain. The people erected a huge tent on the basketball court and set up a wood stove in the middle. The following year, Gennady traveled to America. We traveled from church to church telling the story and raised $10,000 for a new furnace.

Now I understood the scoreboard, Home 1 visitors 0!

My time at Riga was closing. My final class had finished and I was walking to the bus and headed for the plane. Then I heard this awful noise coming from my right rear. Mr. Hatchings, Mr. Hatchings! I turned to see a beautiful blonde girl. She did not hesitate, "I want to study at Missouri Baptist University!" My first thought was, "Becky, look what I brought home from Russia!" But I replied, "Good luck and God bless you. My name is on the board, if you write I will do what I can but will make you no promises."

The next week I was speaking at a church and mentioned Irena. One widow woman came forward and said, "My husband left me very well off. If you can get her here I will pay the first year of tuition."

The next week I was speaking at another church and another widow came forth saying, "My husband left me well off. I have a large house and Irena could stay with me."

Little did I know that Irena had been saving for the trip to America for several years? The next week she was on a plane headed for America. Within three weeks, Irena was in college.

Irena now became a woman without a home. The former President Leonid Brezhnev had spread the Russian population to all parts of the empire including the Baltic States. The people in Latvia lost their jobs to Russian loyalist. The Latvia language, currency, and traditions had to comply with the Russian Czar.

Latvia had now won their independence and was telling the Russian people to go home. Because Irena was of Russian parents she could no longer return to her homeland.

She was a woman without a country. She could not travel to Latvia to visit her parents and she could not immigrate to America. What would happen to her upon graduation from college? She could not go home and she could not stay in America. Irena was truly a woman without a country.

Boys from the hood.

Ledell Redmond - the Spinner

CHAPTER 26
THE BOYS FROM THE HOOD
TURNING INTO MEN

The cast of characters: Ledell Redmond (spinner) 15 years old. Ledell is a show off shooting guard. Not a ball hog, but with good reason very confident. What I like about him is that he never stops. He plays every second of every game as if it were his last game. He knows he is good and walks with a swagger. Confidence, I like that!

Ledell Redmond 15 years old Growing into Manhood, you think he is shaving Shooting guard but got caught calling his girl on my cell phone.

The name on his jersey is, "Spinner." If he is wide open at the three point line he smiles while spinning the ball backwards as if he never misses. But with this much time, he misses every shot. I drew his attention to the fact that when he goes up automatically he hits, but when he shows off, he misses. The habit stopped. One of the joys of working with the boys is to see them grow into manhood.

Darris is so fast that when he runs backward The earth's axis spins backwards.

Darius Redmond (The King) 13 years old, a natural athlete. Darius makes me smile every time he plays. He plays with a full heart and has more fakes than a three dollar bill. During the last game he hit 98 percent of his shots including numerous three pointers. Darius stands only about 5'6" but will dribble up to a 6'4" player take a step back, shoot the ball straight up and sink it.

Darius has more fakes than a $3 Dollar Bill.

Donte leaves the gym cleaner than he found it.

He drives the opposition crazy, especially when he gets rebounds that the power forward or center should have gotten. Darius is in on every play. Like his brother Ledell, he never stops.

One Sunday I told a story about a woman in Memphis who was so beautiful she was called the Queen of the South. Two weeks later while giving Darius a ride he said, "If that lady was the Queen of the South, I am the King of the Mid-West." His jersey reads, "The King."

Kevin, our big man can go Kevin stretching before practice right or left. Double threat!

Kevin Bryant (Kong) 16 years old and is our big man. The first day we met I said, "Kevin if you would lie down and roll you would get down court faster than when you run!" Kevin is a general, a ring leader. I had to kick him off the team for bad language, fighting, poor attitude, and for being born. Two days later, he was pimping on the street corner. While driving by I found him and told him to get in, we would get something to eat.

Kevin got in the car wearing long gold necklace and shades. He immediately said, "George how do you like me pimping on the corner." I waited until we got to Jack in the Box where I could look him in the eye. I will never forget he was taking a bite of his burger as I looked him in the eye and said, "In five years you will be either dead or incarcerated." He dropped his burger. Kevin had been in trouble with the law and there were several business establishments that he was no longer allowed to enter. He heard in my words the ring of truth.

I asked, "Do you want to play ball my way." He said yes, finished the burger and has been making huge personality changes since. He is not a choir boy but he is changing. I love this kid.

And his basketball game is in the paint. His weight keeps him from getting up and down the court but I put him in the paint and he scores. I tell him just stay there; the game will be back in a minute.

The movie, "King Kong," has highly spiritual under tones. The players needed King Kong." After discussing the movies spiritual level, I put on Kevin's jersey, "Kong." He said, "Because I'm big?" I replied, "No, because you can be a giant." He smiled and now gets up and down the court. He is becoming a full player on and off the court.

Donte Gordon seen here cleaning up. We always leave a place in better condition Than when we found it.

Donte Gordon (Shaker). He is the shaker because he will dribble around the top of the three point circle until he shakes loose and then pops his shot. He hits about 8 of 10. The Shaker never stops talking. He complains until we drop the ball and turn the lights out. Sometimes I stop the car and let him out so he can walk home talking to himself. He talks so much he forgets he has the ball.

In my office is the wall of fame. Every time a player does something good, I hang it on the wall. Donte graduated from truancy class and received a diploma. He was so proud that he graduated that I hung it on the wall of fame.

These boys make up the nucleus of the team having stayed with me for two years. I call them my boys. Each player gives me something making me proud. Ledell was the first to complete my program while maintaining good grades. He is now a sophomore and starting player on the McClure South high school basketball team.

On any given day there will be 20 or more players giving me what it takes to succeed on or off the court. I now have a tutoring program.

GEORGE P. HUTCHINGS - COMBAT SURVIVAL

After school they come to my office for homework. No basketball before the home work is done.

April 2004, Christ Memorial Baptist Church became my church home. It came equipped with an empty basketball gym. The church is located in North St. Louis County in a predominately black area. As I drove the streets and kids were everywhere.

So, I got a basketball and went bouncing it down the street. Kids came from everywhere. I asked, "Do you fight or play ball?" They assured me that played ball. Then my question became, "Would you like to play in a gym?" Twenty kids followed me up to the church gym. The first thing that happened was they broke out into a fight. I cleared the gym and went to the street and got some different kids.

After waiting a couple of days, the original group was found and the conversation went something like this. "Isn't it more fun to play in the gym? All we expect is that you not cuss and fight just play ball." They agreed and back to the gym we went.

It has been my pleasure to coach and play basketball with these kids. When bringing the ball down the court they would argue with each other. They would argue to the point that they forgot to dribble the ball and the other team would score. These kids would argue even when they agreed. In my heart I called them, "The Bad News Bears."

How do I make a team out of this? How could I introduce them to faith? How could I turn them into men? I was Coach Carter before Coach Carter was a movie.

The team needed a name and I named them The Breakers. In basketball there is a play called the fast break and that is where I got the name.

However, the real reason for the name is because they broke everything they touched.

The boys came into my office where there was an antique telephone stand. It was fragile and decorative. Everything in my office has a story, and that table had a story. But a 250 pound boy broke it when he rested his oversize butt. My cry went out, "Can't I have anything that isn't broken."

I had a camera on my desk, a player picked up and it immediately dropped. Of course, it broke. It was Christmas Time and I had $300 in my overcoat pocket designated for my family. The coat hung on the coat rack and I went to the men's room. After class, I noticed the money was gone. The players had fought so much that the lesson was, "Turn the other cheek." I had to practice what I preached and announced that all was forgiven, come back and play. I know the culprit but he never returned.

One boy left my office rather angry and slammed the door. My favorite picture fell from the shaken wall and the frame broke. Our team name is, "The Breakers."

I bought 20 new basketballs, they have all disappeared. Stragglers, those boys who are not on the team but take advantage of open gym had bounced the orange toy out the door. The one ball we have has a huge knot in it because someone kicked it instead of throwing. We have four air pumps to inflate flat balls. Someone stole the needles or broke the pumps. If there is something that can't be broke, we break it.

These are boys from the hood. One boy picked up a solid wood chair and chased a kid down the hall. He threw the chair as the boy was going out the steel door. To this day there is the hunk of an old chair leg stopping up a hole from the middle of the hollow steel door.

GEORGE P. HUTCHINGS - COMBAT SURVIVAL

He was told not to return. After a few days, I went to see him and we worked an anger management program. He returned to the gym by breaking out a window at mid-night. I had to go get him out of jail. Nope, I just let him sit.

Every time I spied this boy he was in a fight. He was small but stocky and strong. He also had a winning disposition. We talked and he was invited back. This time he picked up a bigger boy and tried to flush the players head down the commode. It was the unforgivable sin, he is gone.

The first year with the boys was pure hell. Four riots broke out in the gym, and I was thankful for my Marine Corps background. I cleared the gym. On one occasion the fight followed to the parking lot. I had to call the police. The police dispersed the crowd but I had to take two boys home because they were out of the jurisdiction.

The car conversation went something like this: "I hope you know that you have forfeited all your remaining tournament games." Kevin, my big boy, and Dante both started to whine. "It was our fault, let them play and we sit out." I said, "No, you don't understand. What one member of the team does, they all do." Kevin pleaded that I take them to the other boys for a peace party. I did.

The other group of ten did not want to forfeit and the two groups made peace. I said, "It is not that easy!" I need fifty laps. We went to the gym but another team had it rented and my boys thought the punishment would be later. I said, "Nope, 25 laps up and down the three flights of stairs."

Some of the boys tried to sand bag the run but I singled them out for more laps. The sand baggers had to run extra laps, but not just the sand baggers, everyone. We suddenly had a team spirit.

One of my favorite training antics was to play each kid one on one. The kid's age ranged from 12 to 16 and they have all been hooping on the play ground. They had game. I am 59 years old trying to keep up with teenagers! What am I thinking? But what they didn't know was that I play full court each morning with men half my age. The conversation went something like this, "One on one?" They would reply, "But you are an old man." I would say, "Then let us play for blood." "If you beat me what do you want (usually a hamburger) and if I beat you, you come to my Sunday school class." I beat them all hands down and had 10 kids in class.

The real fun came after the victory. I would say, "Do you know who just beat you?" "No." I am three times your age and don't even have a hip, it was shot off in Vietnam and I would show the scars on my right leg. The geriatrics department beat you. Oh! I'm sorry; you don't know what that means. The nursing home just beat you.

It was mid-summer and we were playing full court. It was so hot the birds were laying eggs on the side walk so they could have fried eggs for breakfast. The boys removed their shirts and I followed suit. They had never seen such a white man. Kevin lumbered over and whispered in my ear, "Casper." I knew I was in.

One evening in November 2006 the boys loaded my car to see Darius play his first junior varsity game. After the game we stopped to eat and Darius made a comment: "My Momma told me that some day I would meet a nice white man." Then looking me right in the eye he said, "But it hasn't happened yet!" We laughed all the way home.

When Sunday school is not Sunday school: On Sunday morning I start the rounds picking up 7 or 8 kids. They were each being reared by a single mother and seldom stayed at the same house two nights in a row.

I had to find the crypt. Upon entering the house I would find six kids sleeping on the floor in one bedroom. It was time for the water. To the kitchen sink I would draw a glass of water and throw it on their faces.

Dirty dishes and last nights supper was on the kitchen table. They had eaten white bread with maple syrup. They needed some food! Off to Jack-N-the Box. We often went to Kryspy Kreme Doughnuts. Class took place right there. Each morning I would have one verse and we would memorize it together. The next week we had to remember the previous weeks verse and memorize a new verse.

Because of the constant fighting the first verse was: "Blessed are the peacemakers because they shall be called the sons of God." In time the boys went from being trouble makers to peacemakers. Kevin, the group general, even wrote on his shirt, peacemaker. One week, I took the boys to a St. Charles upscale subdivision. They loved those houses. The verse for the week became, "Without a vision the people perish for lack of knowledge." They needed a vision of something better and than the hammer. The only thing keeping you from having a house like this is your grades. You see these houses are for folks that make A's.

I took the boys to see movies like "King Kong" and "The Last Spear." They loved the Christian parallels I could draw. They could watch a movie at a deeper level.

Many times the kids came to my house, they love Becky's cooking. But they hate having no phone after 9 P.M. and no television after mid-night. We have beds for them, but they all sleep on the living room floor.

One evening after a great basketball victory it was time for Jack-in-the Box. Kevin went in with his pants hanging below his butt and we got kicked out. A deal was struck; my daughter would teach them the manners needed to take a woman to a real restaurant. If they passed the class, I would be their driver. I would pick them and their girl up and take them to any restaurant they wanted. But they had to pay the fare. It was a great success. On December 14, 2006 I finally got to make good on being the driver. I picked up Ledell and his girl friend. They went to a movie and had dinner. I stayed in the car to work on this book!

On the way home I stopped the car on a deserted street in The Hood and went for a walk. Upon arriving back at the car I found Ledell and his girl was hugging. I opened the back door and flipped Ledell the keys and said, "Take us home." The boys now enter business establishments carrying themselves like men and not like thugs. My boys are making me proud.

For two years, I have lived with these kids. We have had over 50 in the gym in one evening. During a recent tournament we had three hundred players using our gym every weekend.

Currently, the gym is packed every night with numerous coaches and teams. What started as a hand full of kids from The Hood has turned into a community center filled with coaches and teams where life disciplines are honed.

The first year the team won second place in the conference.

From left to right beginning in the back row: These boys have been with me from the beginning. Ledell,, Justin, Byrun, Kevin, Scotty, Darris and Dante

In 2006 the team won 11 games and lost 1. They won first place in conference play.

GEORGE P. HUTCHINGS - COMBAT SURVIVAL

You should know that these kids are not choir boys. On trips home there will be eight boys in my four seat car. Farting contest are constant and they even have a song, "Sanitation, come on!" We all roll down the windows. Those boys should be proud of those bodily noises. It is the silencers that get me.

And women, every time we see a woman the whole car howls and screams. The windows down and you would think the car was having a cosmic organism. The Rap music is immediately sought after and I keep finding a way to dodge it. The baseball game, there is too much noise for radio and talk. Any excuse will work, including no!

These are a few of my boys. After working with them for two years five boys have made their freshman team at McClure South High School. This means their grades are acceptable and the game is good.

There is one disappointment. It servers no purpose to embarrass the player by mentioning his name, but one boy has been kicked out of school. He has straight F's. When the news came to me I was a disappointed man. This boy can do well in life but is throwing his life away. My rule is that if you are not in school you don't play. He is off the team.

The Marine Corps taught me that you never allow your buddies to bleed to death on the battle field. You go out and get them. The Bible has a story about a Sheppard who has 100 sheep and one goes astray. The Sheppard searches until the one that who was lost is found. I cannot be content to cut him from the team, I must "Stand in the Gap" and go find him.

The Church no longer has a fund to support this ministry. The program had to be cut without giving thought as to how the church would continue to minister to these youth.

Eagle Wing Ministries now puts out the plea for assistance and the program continues. Much to my delight, many people from the church send checks; we stand together never allowing our men to bleed to death on the battle field.

The following poem was sent to our Pastor Bill Little. It was written by Ryan Tow who committed murder and is serving a life sentence in a penitentiary. He grew up one block from the church. The poem, written February 7, 2005, speaks:

"Empty yet Full"
By Bryan Tow
Time to think, what more did I need?
It's this time I think of all my selfish deeds,
And it's this time I realize its God I need.
It's so simple...why couldn't I see?
I mean he wakes me up every morning and I'd just
Ignore his plea.
What in the world was wrong with me?
I knew better than to let days go by and not
Wander why,
Why did I feel so empty; what's my purpose
Before I die?
Then it hits me, I don't really have to try,
Eventually I break down and can't help but cry.
I mean what other friend do I have that always
By my side, always here to help, and forever here to guide.
Now I close my eyes,
God forgive my ignorance and forgive my sins,
For you I am thankful for all life beginning and end
You are an awesome God and I accept you in my heart.
With your guidance in my life, I will realize my part.
Even though my world seemed dark and cold,
I know now there is plenty to be thankful for,
Amen

GEORGE P. HUTCHINGS - COMBAT SURVIVAL

"God desires a man who will stand in the Gap." That is my ministry to Boys in the Hood, standing between them death or jail. The Old Testament tells of a battle where Moses would raise his hands and the battle would prevail. As the arms of Moses tired and his arms fell the enemy would prevail. The people of Israel would send people to hold the arms of Moses high until victory was won. Now, my arms get tired.

In 2006, due to my community work, Mayor Randy Toles held my arms high by appointing me the Chaplain of the Cool Valley Police Department. While sitting the chief's office a call came in concerning three area youth. The boys ordered water at Jack-N-the-Box and then stole soft drinks. I told the Chief, I know those boys. The police were dispatched to break things up. The manager told the kids they could not come back on the premises.

Chad lived about five blocks from the fast food restaurant and was one of my new players. I drove out to pick him up and said, "Let's go get something to eat." He jumped in my car and I headed for Jack. Upon parking in the lot, I said, "Oh, you can't go in here anymore. You were stealing drinks." Chad said, "No, not me that was the others."

"Chad, then you are guilty by association, you can't go in here and you are named as a thief, and your father is named a thief and I am named a thief because I am your coach. But there is one thing called restitution.

If you were to walk the parking lot, pick up all the trash, and then go in with me, all might be forgiven." He did, they did, and we had that lunch. The process was completed three times and the boys now walk in like a man, order their lunch and then clean their tables making things better than when they arrived. What did the Old Testament Prophet say, "God desires a man who will stand in the gap."

Smile! Remember my boy with the straight F's and who was out of school? He is sitting at my breakfast table doing his homework. :)

Back in school, all the sheep are in the flock and none have died on the battlefield.

The Breakers go 11-1, winning 1st Place in their conference!

CHAPTER 27
KENYA, THE ONLY PLACE

In American, I don't have a voice. There are overwhelming competing voices; television evangelist, baseball, hotdogs, apple pie and Chevrolet. America is a nation consumed with wealth and sports. We have in the name of tolerance asked God to leave our classrooms, homes, and career choices. My voice is silenced; even the churches have invited God to leave so they can build their own budgets and programs. Even when a church gives birth to a new ministry, very few churches will even acknowledge the effort as coming from God.

The people who listen to me in America are the street boys, bar owners, and prostitutes. And that is the audience that needs me.

But in Kenya, I can, "Lift up my voice like a Trumpet." People hear and believe. My impotence in America is a force in Kenya. Since 1999 Eagle Wing Ministries has shipped over two million dollars of medical supplies and have arranged for over 100 surgeries for children with huge tumors on their head.

In Kenya, I have talked with The President and the Poor. The full range of society is open to the faith message.

In March 2005 a lady named Valery Hays called me. She had a passion for the people of Kenya and her pastor gave my referral. Her family met me at Denney's for breakfast and the odds were overwhelming that she would ever travel to the land of mountains, wild beast, and orphans. The family and work situation were such that going to Kenya was impossible. In a faith moment, I said bring the whole family, kids and all. And so it was.

GEORGE P. HUTCHINGS - COMBAT SURVIVAL

We arrived in Kenya July 2005 and Valery immediately found three orphanages: Hosanna House, El Shadi, and God of Mercy and Grace. The children were orphans due to AIDS, tribal wars, and refugees from the Sudan and Somalia.

The children wore rags and Valery with the help of Hanna Woods School in West County, St. Louis where she is a counselor, had raised the funds to provide 150 children with school uniforms. It was winter time and kids were running around with no shoes. I cried.

Another problem was the cooking. The fuel was charcoal that fumed carbon dioxide into the air. Everyone had respiratory problems. Bob was on call again and we provided gas cookers to replace the charcoal.

The people of Kenya have the most loving disposition. If they do not have a bed, they thank God for a blanket. If they do not have a blanket, they thank God for a roof over their head.

Orphanages spring up spontaneously. Children roam the streets and slums until a caring person takes them into their home. Then more children find their way to that caring heart and suddenly their home expands into a school with room and board. The children are wearing rags, no shoes, and are starving. Of course, the school has no books. In spite of hardships the children are happy and the headmasters demonstrate the most caring hearts.

Valery asked each orphanage what their number one need was. They all replied, "A Cow." With a cow they could have milk and butter and sell the excess. With the extra money they could purchase other food products. An attractive site at each orphanage was that each child had chores to do and they all kept a garden. Discipline was not a problem.

Two weeks after arriving back home Eagle Wings with the help of Valery raised the $1500 to purchase the cows.

In July of 2006 Bob Hack, Valery Hays and I make our 2006 pilgrimage. We saw the cows and each had caved.

Bob is a man who can fix anything and Valery is a consular in the Parkways school district.

Each orphanage is an enclosed compound with a 14 foot security wall surrounding the kids and staff. Hosanna House had a problem with security. The gate had been compromised and men from the village would sneak in at night and rape the kids. Bob and Valery had raised additional funds and a new iron gate was purchased. Bob knew how to anchor it to the concrete structure. The kids and staff are now secure.

The Headmaster at Hosanna House told us they had problems with drug dealers and prostitutes. I asked, "Where are they; that is my kind of people?" The Headmaster pointed to the next street up. Much to their surprise, I walked out of the compound headed for the next street. The Headmaster was worried about my safety and had a local pastor follow me. It was a good idea because I needed someone to interpret.

I talked to individuals and drew a crowd. My question to my new friends was; "Do you know Jesus?" Some said, "Yes." My reply then became, "Do you know about him or do you know him?" The street people asked me to give them a conference. The conference was scheduled for the next day at 10 AM. Forty people came to the orphanage. I shook hands, hugged them, played with the kids, sang songs and then preached. Four drug dealers came forward changing their lives. These former drug dealers later sought me out with the testimony that their faith continued.

GEORGE P. HUTCHINGS - COMBAT SURVIVAL

The next day thirty (30) more people came and three more people repented activating their faith.

In 2007, one of the greatest needs is an outhouse. In the area of hygiene the only bathroom they know is a hole in the ground. They squat with naked feet on soiled ground to use the bathroom. Each year the kids must be de-wormed because their feet offer pores for mites and worms to enter their bodies.

On the left, the traditional hole had no privacy or stool. Bob Heck built the new model with privacy doors and a stool. We have three more to build.

In December 2007, a Dr. Gil Hart donated a dental chair, instrument including x-ray machines and cabinets. Derma Sciences has donated ten skids of medical supplies. Today, I received a request that Eagle Wings help establish a library equipped with internet capability. I am praying for 10,000 books and funds for the internet request. This is funny: a town so far into the mountains that they receive only one television channel and most people do not have electricity or televisions. But there are limited phone lines and with internet they will be connected to the rest of the world.

On December 14, 2007 a computer and twelve cases of books have been donated for the library. And Brown Shoe Company is donating 1000 pairs of shoes!

In the beginning my cry was, "Any place but Africa." Now my cry is, "There is no place like Kenya." My ministry plans are domestic and foreign. While in St. Louis, I will work with, "The Boys from the Hood." And in Kenya, every year is a new challenge. In 1990 God gave me the promise that in my old age, when I can no longer run, but only walk, He will have a work for me and I will not faint. So far, his promise has been true. I run with, "The Boys in the Hood," and walk with the, "The Souls in Kenya."

GEORGE P. HUTCHINGS - COMBAT SURVIVAL

EPILOGUE

Jesus was the first Marine

In his book, The Struggle of the Soul, Lewis Joseph Sherrill wrote:

"Providence presents one with a crisis. One either draws back, in which case, 'His soul will find no pleasure,' or he proceeds, trusting fate, in which case purpose is found. Purpose is the motivation for all life. Life without purpose is death. Crisis is the situation through which purpose expresses itself. A crisis is not always bad. In fact, crisis is what allows man to 'Rise to the occasion.' It is necessary for life. A pump handle is to a well what a crisis is to life."

When one's purpose is only on a horizontal level, man with man, the purpose will fail. Governments, relatives, work-they all fail at some time or another. Therefore, a vertical relationship must be the source of one's purpose; else we pass from day to day, only to die like the animal kingdom. God intersects that horizontal line with His vertical presence, like the upright beam of a cross, and gives man the challenge to look up and live!

God told Moses long ago to cross the Jordan River into the Promised Land. Ten spies were sent out to find a plan. Looking only at the enemy they had to defeat, they drew back, being afraid. God confronted man with a crisis. Either follow on in faith or draw back. In this case, they drew back by majority rule. For forty years they wandered in the wilderness and died, for "His soul would have no pleasure in them."

Forty years later, God confronted man with the very same crisis.

GEORGE P. HUTCHINGS - COMBAT SURVIVAL

This time they looked up and Joshua led them in victory over Jericho. Purpose for life comes only when we go forth, trusting an invisible vertical hand.

In 1994, subsequent to the events of this book, and after many more wilderness experiences, I was given yet another opportunity from a gracious Savior to "follow on in faith or draw back." The only choice was to follow, founding Eagle Wing Ministries.

The new ministry had one purpose: To go through every door that opens, touching lives with the grace of God. Touching lives might mean learning sign language, financing ministry work for others, hauling hamburger warmers, feeding orphans, providing a college education for students who would otherwise never have the opportunity, making the attendant at Quick Trip laugh with encouragement, or raising funds for a new college dormitory. Eagle Wings has done all of these.

The word "ministries" is used as a flexible term, allowing new methods and avenues of approach to bring God's Spirit to the hearts of people. People are a union of body, mind, and spirit. Impact on any one of these is felt through all three. In every outreach of Eagle Wings, discovering the point of need within this union makes the ministry relevant. As the ministry becomes relevant it provides a seed of faith that nourishes the whole person. "If a man has faith the size of a mustard seed, he can move mountains." Jesus.

Sometimes finding the point of need involves learning a new language. In North St. Louis basketball is the language of The Hood. Basketball is the common denominator that builds relationships. A relationship is the rail road track upon which a faith ministry rolls.

Early in the ministry, while teaching at The Riga International Bible Institute in Riga, Latvia, Irena Salaban approached me with a plea for study in St. Louis. Reluctant to make promises, I replied, "Good luck and God bless. My address is on the board. Write to me, but I will not promise."

After returning to the states, Irena's need was mentioned at a local church and an elderly woman approached me, "My husband has left me pretty well off, I will pay her first year of tuition if you can get her here." The next week another senior lady approached him and said, "My husband left me a big house. If you can get her here she will have a place to stay." A scholarship ministry was born! "And now for the rest of the story"-Paul Harvey. Subsequently, six scholarships were provided through the ministry.

Eagle Wing Ministries has become a ministry that finds people stuck and lifts them to the next level. In 2006, Eagle Wings gave birth to a new ministry, "Mercies Hope." Mercies Hope works with orphans in Kenya even to the level of creating a college opportunity.

In 1994 the word Wing was used in the ministry name because I found myself working alone. But, in the back of my mind I knew there would be another that would join him. This person, who was yet to be met, would add the second wing, and the bird would fly as Eagle Wings. In 1998, John Kihumba of Kenya became that second wing. John and I became Eagle Wings and their first landing was in 1999 with the delivery of over $100,000 worth of medical supplies to Kenya's neediest.

In 2001, Eagle Wings shipped to Kenya much needed medical supplies for surgeons at Washington University School of Medicine. This equipment had to arrive in time to be used by neurosurgeons to perform lifesaving surgeries for children with large brain tumors.

The equipment arrived on the day the surgeons were to begin their operations. To this date over 112 surgeries have been performed.

Since that day in 1973 when my faith moved from dormant to active I have learned that man cannot give God conditions. If the Lord wants a man in Africa, a path will be created. Oh! I forgot. Did you know Jesus was the first Marine? He said, "I will never leave you nor forsake you, nor leave you comfortless." He says, "Come and follow me." This creates a conflict or crisis. Am I afraid to follow the invisible hand? Christ says, "Come and follow me." Not in a physical sense, but in the spiritual. His greatest lesson was "Love your enemies, do good to those who despitefully use you and persecute you."

This is quite different from the Muslim clerics who sent out suicide bombers and called them martyrs. A martyr is one who is killed for his faith, not one who kills himself and others. This also causes a crisis. My question is simple: Why do the Muslim clerics say go kill yourself and others and you will received 72 virgins? What if Allah is out of virgins? And why do the clerics say, "Go, instead of follow me into death!" Jesus said, "Follow me." Jesus went first and now asks us to live for him, not die.

Jesus was the real thing. The crisis is: Are you willing to follow the truth: Allah or Jesus?

Christ has a path that he puts you on, will you stay on that path or try to run the other way? Jonah tried to run the other way, but God created a great fish to correct his course. So pilgrim, get ready for a great ride forward, never looking back.

In the prologue I said that the Marines have a motto, "Semper Fi." This could be built on scripture.

This means they will never allow their buddies to bleed to death on the battlefield. Jesus said, "I will never leave you nor forsake you nor leave you comfortless. Jesus was the first Marine. Semper Fi - always faithful.

If you would like more information concerning this ministry the web site is: www.EagleWingMinistries.org

Printed in the United States
73125LV00005B/145-231